Emma O'Reilly

Emma O'Reilly

FIRST
FUN
HISTORY
ENCYCLOPEDIA

First published in 2004 by
Miles Kelly Publishing Ltd
Bardfield Centre
Great Bardfield
Essex CM7 4SL

2 4 6 8 1 0 9 7 5 3 1

British Library Cataloguing-in-Publication Data
A catalogue record for this book is available from the British Library

ISBN 1-84236-300-X

Printed in China

Project Editor
Amanda Learmonth

Assistant Editor
Nicola Sail

Copy Editor
Sarah Ridley

Designers
Robert Walster, Debbie Meekcoms

Picture Researcher
Bethany Walker

Proofreader
Ann Kay

Indexer
Jane Parker

Production Manager
Estela Godoy

www.mileskelly.net
info@mileskelly.net

FIRST FUN HISTORY ENCYCLOPEDIA

Philip Steele

Miles KeLLY
PUBLISHING

Contents

How to use this book

Your *First Fun History Encyclopedia* is bursting with information, colour pictures and fun activities. The pages run from A to Z with a new subject on every page. This will help you find information quickly and easily. There are comic cartoons to bring amazing true facts to life and puzzles and games to tease your brain. The index at the back of the book will help you look for specific information.

Colour bands

Your encyclopedia has six subject areas. The coloured bands along the top of each page tell you which area of history you are in.
• Prehistory (before 10,000BC) has red bands.
• Ancient World (10,000BC to AD500) has green bands.
• Middle Ages (AD500 to 1450) has blue bands.
• Ages of Discovery (1500s to 1800s) has yellow bands.
• Modern World (1800s to present day) has orange bands.
• General History has purple bands.

Orange Wow boxes

Look for the orange panels to read amazing true facts – the funny cartoons will make you laugh!

Yellow Word boxes

New or difficult words are explained in the yellow panels.

Alphabet strip

Your book is alphabetical. This means it runs from A to Z. Along the bottom of every page is an alphabet strip. The letter that starts the main heading is in bold. Above the letter there's a small arrow to highlight where you are in the alphabet.

Ancient Roman Empire

Find c
Ancient R

▲ The power of Rome

The Romans conquered Greece and Egypt. Soon they ruled all the lands from sunny Spain to the deserts of Syria, from rainy Britain to the mountains of North Africa.

▲ High arches

Roman cities had paved streets with gutters and drains. Pipes and channels called aqueducts carried fresh water into the cities.

▼ Straight roads

Roman engineers built the best roads the world had ever seen. They were made of stone and followed a straight line from one city to the next

large stone slabs

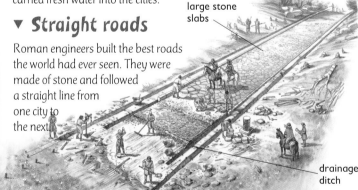

drainage ditch

Rome was the centre of the w
Or this is how it seemed to people in
2,000 years ago. From small beginni
Italian city grew and grew. It became
centre of a huge empire. Roman pow
until AD476, when the city was capture
German warriors.

▶ Julius Caesar

Julius Caesar was the most famous Roman soldier of all time. He conquered Gaul (France) and attacked Britain. He became the leader of the Romans, but some people were jealous of his power and they murdered him, in 44BC.

Wow!

The Romans set aside 135 days of each year for holidays and festivals that's more than one third of a year!

Word bc

empire
many different land
ruled by one cou

legion
a unit of the Roman c
up of about 5,500 mo
and foot sold

Main text
Every page begins with a paragraph of main text on each subject.

Cross-references
Within the colour band are cross-references to other subjects. These tell you where you can find more information about your chosen topic. Follow the arrows to turn backwards or forwards to the correct page.

Pictures
Illustrations or photographs accompany each caption. Many illustrations are labelled to explain what different parts of them are called.

Ancient Roman life

Find out more:
Ancient Roman Empire ◄ Clothes ►
Disasters ► Food ►

The city of Rome had bustling streets, crowded blocks of flats, markets, theatres, public baths and stadiums for horse-racing. Out in the country, rich people lived in fancy houses called villas. Some of these even had central heating! Roman farmers grew crops such as wheat, olives and grapes.

◄ At the baths

Every town in the Roman Empire had public baths. These ones in Bath, England, can still be seen. People came here to meet their friends, to have a hot or a cold dip, or perhaps a massage with oil.

▲ Cruel combat

The Colosseum was a big arena in Rome. Up to 50,000 people could pack into the stands. They loved to watch trained fighters called gladiators battle to the death.

Jupiter   Juno

► Gods and thunderbolts

The Romans worshipped many different gods. Jupiter was the father of them all. He could send thunderbolts whizzing across the sky. Juno, his wife, was goddess of marriage. Their son was Mars, god of war.

▼ Dinner time

The Romans' main meal was in the evening. Diners lay on couches around a low table. Pork, veal or goose might be on the menu – or, for a special treat, fat little dormice or flamingo tongues!

Captions
Captions give you detailed information about all the photographs and illustrations in your book.

Make a mosaic

The Romans made floor pictures called mosaics from many little coloured tiles.

1. Cut out small squares of brightly coloured paper.

2. Arrange them to make a picture and stick them on to a large piece of card.

Activity and puzzle boxes
Some pages will have activities, games or puzzles for you to do. Look for the green or blue panels.

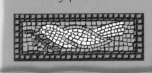

a b c d e f g h i j k l m n o p q r s t u v w x y z **15**

African kingdoms

For hundreds of years, people outside Africa knew little of its people or the place. Africa was difficult to explore, with huge forests, vast rivers and deserts to cross. Merchants and explorers heard rumours of kingdoms ruled by great chiefs. Many of these kingdoms really existed. Their peoples lived by hunting and farming, or by trading.

▶ Circle of stone

Between the 1000s and the 1400s, the Shona people of southern Africa were mining gold and making cotton cloth. They built a royal palace at Great Zimbabwe. Its huge stone walls still stand today.

▲ Fighting force

Few warriors could stand up to the armies of the Zulu people. They conquered large areas of South Africa in the 1820s. Their fighters carried spears, shields and wooden clubs.

▼ Statue of a hero

Legends from central Africa tell of Chibinda Ilunga, who lived in the 1500s. He was a prince of the Luba people but fell in love with Lweji, a Lunda princess. He came to rule over her nation and was wise and just.

▲ Mosque at Mali

In the 1300s, the West African empire of Mali was famous for its fabulous riches. Its merchants crossed the Sahara Desert by camel, travelling all the way to North Africa. These merchants were Muslims who worshipped in religious buildings such as this one, called mosques.

American Revolution

How did the USA begin?

During the 1600s and 1700s, many people from the British Isles settled in North America. The places where they made their new homes were called colonies. These were ruled by Britain. In the 1770s, people living in the colonies rose up against the British. They wanted their freedom.

▲ What a tea party!

The people of Boston were fed up with paying money to the British government and getting nothing in return. They even had to pay a tax on tea. In 1773, in protest, some colonists crept on board three British ships, wearing disguises. They threw the cargoes of tea into the harbour!

▼ First president

The rebel army had been led by a soldier called George Washington. In 1789 he became the first president of the United States.

▲ The war begins

In 1775, a man called Paul Revere discovered that British soldiers were marching to a village called Lexington to capture rebels there. He rode all night to warn them. When the British finally reached the village, the rebels were ready for them. The battle that followed sparked off the War of Independence.

◀ A free country

In 1776, the American rebels declared that the colonies were independent from British rule. The war continued but by 1781 the British had lost. A new country called the United States of America had been born.

Word box

independence
freedom from rule by another country

tax
money which people have to pay to a government, so that it can run the country

Ancient Egyptian life

Find out more:
Ancient Egyptian tombs ▶

Egypt became a powerful kingdom about 5,000 years ago. Its rulers were called pharaohs. The ancient Egyptians built great cities, pyramids, statues and temples. Some of them can still be seen today. The ancient Egyptians used a kind of picture-writing and made paper called papyrus from reeds.

▲ Marvellous mud

Floods from the river Nile left behind thick, black mud. This was the perfect soil for growing wheat, barley and vegetables. Egyptian farmers also raised cattle, sheep, pigs and geese.

▶ Water works

This machine is called a *shaduf*. The ancient Egyptians used it to lift water from the river Nile. They needed water for their crops, because there was hardly any rainfall. Egypt is a baking-hot land with sandy deserts.

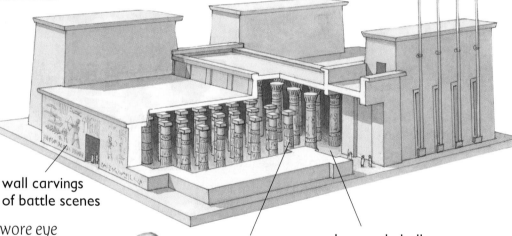

wall carvings
of battle scenes

decorated
columns

hypostyle hall
where processions
took place

◀ Fashion and beauty

Ancient Egyptian women wore eye make-up and lipstick. Both men and women wore jewellery and wigs. Men wore a simple tunic or kilt, while women wore long dresses of white linen.

▲ Praise to Amun-ra!

The temple of Karnak is massive. Its priests worshipped a god called Amun-ra around 4,000 years ago. Each New Year they held a big festival there. They killed oxen and offered them to the god.

▶ Pharaoh power

This pharaoh was called Rameses II. He ruled Egypt over 3,000 years ago. People believed that the pharaohs were gods living on Earth.

Ancient Egyptian tombs

Find out more:
Ancient Egyptian life ◄

Magic spells and curses were used to protect ancient Egyptian tombs. At first, the pharaohs were buried inside huge stone tombs called pyramids, which pointed up to the sky. Later, they were buried secretly in rock tombs, hidden in the Valley of the Kings, near the ancient city of Thebes.

▲ World wonders

Three huge pyramids can still be seen at Giza, near Cairo. The biggest one is made of over two million heavy blocks of stone! It was built for a pharaoh called Khufu, who died in 2566BC.

Isis
Osiris
Horus

▲ Gods and death

The ancient Egyptians worshipped thousands of different gods and goddesses. Three of the most important ones were Osiris, the god of death and his wife Isis, maker of the first mummy. Horus was their son, and protector of the pharaoh.

Wow!
The Egyptians made mummies of animals, including cats, birds and crocodiles.

▲ King Tut's tomb

A young pharaoh called Tutankhamun died in 1327BC. He was buried in the Valley of the Kings. His tomb was packed with gold and all sorts of fantastic treasure. This was for him to use in the next life, or afterlife.

▶ Making mummies

Egyptians wanted their bodies to stay whole after they died, so that they would be able to travel to the next world. Trained people removed the internal organs first. Then they dried out the body, rubbed it with oils and wrapped it in bandages. The body was placed inside a wooden coffin.

Dolphins leap through sparkling blue seas.
Women shake their black, curly hair. Servants carry jugs of wine. All these scenes appear in wall paintings found in ancient palaces on the Greek island of Crete. They show us what it was like to live in Greece between about 3000BC and 1100BC.

▼ Stone cities

Kings in the south of Greece built stone forts called citadels. This one was at a place called Mycenae. It contained a royal palace, as well as houses for soldiers and craftsmen. It was surrounded by a stone wall.

city walls

store rooms for food

royal palace

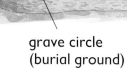

the Lion Gate was the main gateway, decorated with two stone lions

grave circle (burial ground)

houses

▲ Monster in the maze

Greek myths tell how a terrifying monster lived on Crete in an underground maze called the labyrinth. He was believed to be half-man, half-bull and was called the Minotaur.

▼ The Wooden Horse

For years the Greeks tried to capture the city of Troy, in what is now Turkey. Finally, they came up with a plan. They built a big wooden horse, and left it outside the city walls. A few of the Greek soldiers hid inside, while the rest sailed away. Puzzled, the people of Troy hauled the horse into the city. Little did they know what was hidden inside! The Greek soldiers burst out and attacked everyone.

▲ Thrills and spills

The king of Crete was called the Minos. The nobles at his palace liked to watch acrobats. These young people would somersault over the backs of fierce bulls and leap between their sharp horns.

Ancient Greek cities

Find out more:
Ancient Greek beginnings ◄

After about 800BC, cities began to grow up all over Greece. Each city had its own ruler. In 508BC, the people of Athens decided to be ruled by a group of locals, or citizens. This new idea was called democracy, meaning 'rule by the people'.

Wow!

Alexander the Great used soldiers on elephants to charge at the enemy.

▲ City of the goddess

Athens was named after the goddess of wisdom, Athena. Her temple, the Parthenon, stood on a high rock above the city. The Athenians were great thinkers, poets, artists and craftsmen.

◄ Tough ones

In Sparta, both men and women were trained to be really tough. When a huge Persian army invaded Greece, Spartan soldiers like this one fought to the last man.

▼ To the east

In 334BC, Alexander led a Greek army to capture lands to the east. His soldiers were extremely well-trained. The Greeks conquered Persia and marched on to India. They conquered Egypt, too, where the city of Alexandria is named after him.

▼ A great leader

Alexander the Great, a brilliant soldier, came from Macedonia, in northern Greece. All of Greece came under his rule.

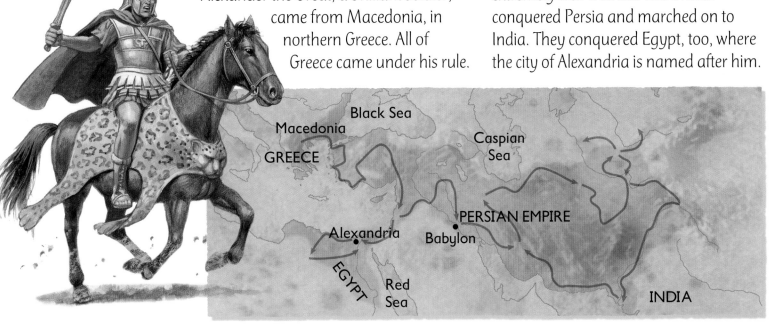

Black Sea
Macedonia
Caspian Sea
GREECE
Alexandria
Babylon
PERSIAN EMPIRE
EGYPT
Red Sea
INDIA

Ancient Roman Empire

Find out more:
Ancient Roman life ▶

Rome was the centre of the world. Or this is how it seemed to people in Europe 2,000 years ago. From small beginnings, this Italian city grew and grew. It became the centre of a huge empire. Roman power lasted until AD476, when the city was captured by German warriors.

▶ Julius Caesar

Julius Caesar was the most famous Roman soldier of all time. He conquered Gaul (France) and attacked Britain. He became the leader of the Romans, but some people were jealous of his power and they murdered him, in 44BC.

▲ The power of Rome

The Romans conquered Greece and Egypt. Soon they ruled all the lands from sunny Spain to the deserts of Syria, from rainy Britain to the mountains of North Africa.

▲ High arches

Roman cities had paved streets with gutters and drains. Pipes and channels called aqueducts carried fresh water into the cities.

◀ On the march

The Roman army was divided into legions. The soldiers wore iron armour and helmets and fought with spears and short swords.

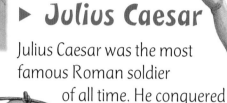

▼ Straight roads

Roman engineers built the best roads. They were made of stone and followed a straight line from one city to the next.

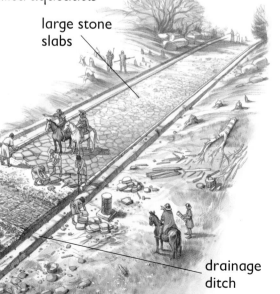

large stone slabs

drainage ditch

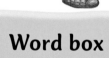

Word box

empire
many different lands that are ruled by one country

legion
a unit of the Roman army, made up of about 5,500 mounted troops and foot soldiers

Ancient Roman life

Find out more:
Ancient Roman Empire ◀ Clothes ▶
Disasters ▶ Food ▶

The city of Rome had bustling streets, crowded blocks of flats, markets, theatres, public baths and stadiums for horse-racing. Out in the country, rich people lived in fancy houses called villas. Some of these even had central heating! Roman farmers grew crops such as wheat, olives and grapes.

◀ At the baths

Every town in the Roman Empire had public baths. These ones in Bath, England, can still be seen. People came here to meet their friends, to have a hot or a cold dip, or perhaps a massage with oil.

▲ Cruel combat

The Colosseum was a big arena in Rome. Up to 50,000 people could pack into the stands. They loved to watch trained fighters called gladiators battle to the death.

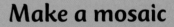

Jupiter   Juno

▶ Gods and thunderbolts

The Romans worshipped many different gods. Jupiter was the father of them all. He could send thunderbolts whizzing across the sky. Juno, his wife, was goddess of marriage. Their son was Mars, god of war.

▼ Dinner time

The Romans' main meal was in the evening. Diners lay on couches around a low table. Pork, veal or goose might be on the menu – or, for a special treat, fat little dormice or flamingo tongues!

Make a mosaic

The Romans made floor pictures called mosaics from many little coloured tiles.

1. Cut out small squares of brightly coloured paper.

2. Arrange them to make a picture and stick them on to a large piece of card.

Anglo-Saxons

Find out more:
Britain and Ireland ▶ Normans ▶ Vikings ▶

Who were the Anglo-Saxons? Their ancestors (relatives from long ago) were people from northern Germany, called Angles, Saxons, Frisians and Jutes. Groups of them invaded southern Britain about 1,500 years ago and set up small kingdoms. Over time, the language they spoke developed into much of the English spoken today.

▼ Village life

The Anglo-Saxons built villages of timber houses with thatched roofs. They farmed the land and raised cattle and sheep. During the AD600s and AD700s many of them became Christians and built stone churches.

▶ Face of war

In about AD625, one Anglo-Saxon warrior was buried in his finest rowing ship, under a big mound of earth. It is thought the warrior may have been Redwald, king of East Anglia. He was buried with his gold coins, his finest jewellery, his prized weapons and this scary-looking helmet made from iron and bronze.

▲ King Alfred of Wessex

In the AD800s the most powerful of the Anglo-Saxon kingdoms was called Wessex. Its wisest king was called Alfred. He built new towns and a fleet of ships. His warriors fought against the Danes, who were invading the north and east of England.

Arabs

The Arabs came from the burning hot deserts of Arabia, in southwest Asia. They lived in tents and herded camels. They also built towns and cities. Between the AD600s and AD900s, Muslim Arabs conquered areas of the Middle East, Africa and Spain. They built beautiful palaces and mosques.

▲ Dome of the Rock

Muslim Arabs captured Jerusalem in AD638. They built this mosque with the golden roof in AD691. Jerusalem remains a holy city to Jews, Christians and Muslims.

▲ Sailing the seas

The Arabs built big wooden sailing ships called dhows. These carried bales of silk and cotton, spices and coffee beans. The Arab merchants traded with East Africa, India, Southeast Asia and China.

▼ Holy words

Arab design and Arab script, or way of writing, were often very beautiful. This is a copy of the *Qur'an* (the Koran), the Muslim holy scriptures.

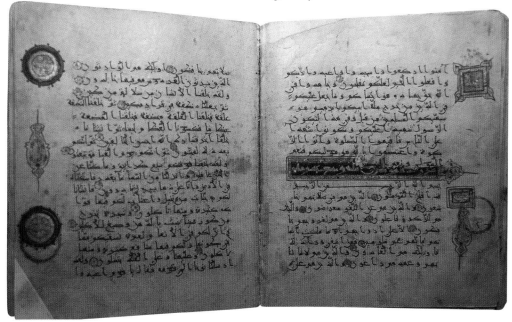

Word box

mosque
a place of worship for Muslims

Muslim
a follower of Islam, the religion of the Prophet Muhammad

Art in history

Find out more:
Music and dance ▶ Theatre and cinema ▶
Writing and printing ▶

People were already drawing and painting pictures thousands of years ago, during the Stone Age. Over the centuries, artists all over the world liked to paint animals, people, gods and goddesses, landscapes, colours and patterns. They learned how to paint on rocks, walls, wood, canvas and paper.

◀ Cave painting

About 17,000 years ago, many people in Europe lived in caves. On the rocks, they painted lively pictures of the animals they hunted. They used paints made of earth or soot.

▼ Splish! Splash! Splosh! Splat!

Jackson Pollock lived in the USA. In the 1950s he used to make paintings with swirling colours by hurling, splattering and dribbling paint across the canvas.

▼ Simple beauty

Japanese art of the 1500s and 1600s was simple and patterned. Artists painted bold, flat shapes, using bright colours and gold leaf (a thin sheet of metal). This picture shows part of a painting used to decorate a paper screen.

▲ Light and colour

Claude Monet was a French painter who lived from 1840 to 1926. Instead of painting every scene in great detail, he chose to paint his impressions of light and colour. He was called an Impressionist.

Word scramble

Can you unscramble these names? They belong to some of the most famous artists in history:

a. ANGCHIMLEOLE
b. MERTDNABR
c. NAV HGGO

answers
a. Michelangelo b. Rembrandt
c. Van Gogh

Asia: Southeast

Southeast Asia is a region of tropical forests and islands. For thousands of years people grew rice and traded with India, China and Arabia. Some became Hindus, Buddhists or Muslims. Powerful kingdoms grew up in Southeast Asia between 1,500 and 700 years ago.

cinnamon

cloves

pepper

▲ Angkor Wat

The world's biggest religious site is called Angkor Wat. This temple was built in honour of the Hindu god Vishnu. It dates back to the 1100s, when the Khmer Empire ruled Cambodia.

▼ Early cinema

Puppets like this one were being used on Java over 900 years ago. They were placed behind a cotton screen and lit from behind. When moved by sticks, they made shadows across the screen. Shadow puppets are still in use today.

▼ Ancient dances

Beautiful dances like these have been seen on the island of Java for hundreds of years. They were first performed at the royal court.

▲ Spice islands

The islands of Southeast Asia produced precious spices. These included pepper, cinnamon bark and the dried flower buds of the clove tree. After the 1500s, merchants from Portugal, Britain and the Netherlands seized control of the trade in spices.

▶ Countries of Southeast Asia

A hundred years ago, most of Southeast Asia was ruled by European countries. About 50 years ago, Southeast Asian countries began to win back their freedom.

CHINA

MYANMAR

THAILAND VIETNAM

CAMBODIA

PHILIPPINES

BRUNEI Pacific Ocean

MALAYA

Singapore

BORNEO

SUMATRA

JAVA Bali

Assyrian Empire

Find out more:
Cities of ancient times ▶

The Assyrians were a mean bunch. Their soldiers were famous for skinning enemies alive! But they were clever scholars, too. They were carvers of stone and builders of roads and cities. Between about 1700BC and 612BC, the Assyrians built up a mighty Middle Eastern empire.

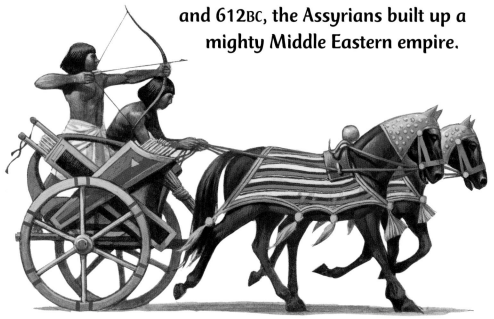

▲ The last king

Ashurbanipal came to the throne in 668BC and set up a great library in the city of Nineveh. He was the last great Assyrian king. After his death there were revolts all over the empire. Nineveh was destroyed in 612BC.

▲ Chariots and bows

Big chariots pulled by three horses were used in war. Some had sharp, whirling knives fixed to the wheels. Assyrian soldiers carried deadly bows and arrows and iron spears and swords.

Wow!

Assyrian soldiers used inflated animal skins to cross deep rivers.

▲ Winged gods

Like the people of Babylon, the Assyrians worshipped gods of earth, fire, wind and water, and winged spirits or genies. The chief god of the Assyrians, shown in this stone engraving, was called Ashur.

◀ Many peoples

The great empire stretched from Egypt and Cyprus in the west to the Persian Gulf in the east. Many different peoples came within its borders.

Australia

The first Australians are called Aborigines. They came to Australia from Southeast Asia over 50,000 years ago. They fished and hunted animals, such as kangaroos and wombats. Dutch explorers sailed along the coasts of Australia in the 1600s. Then, in 1788, British people arrived at Botany Bay and began to settle the land.

◀ Ancient sounds

This Aborigine is playing an ancient instrument called a didgeridoo. Music, dance and storytelling recall the ancient history, beliefs and traditions of the Australian Aborigines.

◀ Ned Kelly

The 1870s were wild and lawless times in Australia. Ned Kelly and his gang of bushrangers stole cattle and robbed banks. When Ned was captured, he was wearing a home-made suit of armour.

▶ A new nation

The British used Australia as a place to send prisoners and to settle free people. They divided the land into separate colonies. Australia became a united country in 1901. This flag, which dates back to 1909, became the official flag of Australia in 1954.

Australia's flag

stars of the Southern Cross

Word box

bushranger
an escaped convict or gangster who lived in Australia in the 1800s

colony
a settlement created in a foreign land by people who have moved away from their own country

◀ Gold and sheep

In the 1800s, more and more Europeans arrived in Australia. They often attacked the Aborigines and forced them off their land. Many of the newcomers were sheep farmers. Others were miners – shown here at a gold mine in Western Australia in 1910.

Aztecs and Mayans

In the 1840s, explorers discovered ruined cities deep in the jungles of Mexico and Central America. They had been built by the ancient peoples of the region, such as the Mayans, whose history stretches back 5,000 years. The Aztec people built the city of Tenochtitlán in the middle of a lake in 1325. It was the capital of a great empire.

► Chichén Itzá

The Mayans built a city at Chichén Itzá over 1,100 years ago. It had massive stone temples like this one. When the Toltec people conquered the Mayans, they built a new city nearby. Chichén Itzá fell into ruins and the jungle grew up around it.

▲ Score!

The Central Americans loved to play a ball game called *tlachtli*. The players on the court had to get a small rubber ball through a stone hoop. The game was fast, rough and very exciting.

Wow!

The peoples of Central America invented chewing gum. It was made from the sap of a tree and was called *chicle*.

► Steps to heaven

The Great Temple towered over Tenochtitlán. It was 60 metres high. Steps led up to two shrines at the top. Here priests worshipped the rain and Sun gods.

Great Temple

▲ Stone giants

Many civilizations grew up in ancient Central America. The Olmec people lived around the Bay of Campeche about 3,000 years ago. They carved huge heads from stone.

Britain and Ireland

Find out more:
Anglo-Saxons ◄ Celts ►
Empires and colonies ► Normans ► Vikings ►

Celts, Anglo-Saxons, Vikings and Normans settled on the islands of Britain and Ireland long ago, and founded small kingdoms. These later grouped together into Ireland, Wales, Scotland and England, and eventually joined to form the United Kingdom (or UK). During the 1800s, people from Britain and Ireland settled in many other parts of the world.

▲ Scotland's might

Parts of Edinburgh Castle are nearly 1,000 years old. Its high walls guarded the kingdom of Scotland from attacks by the English. From 1603 the Scottish king became king of England, too. Scotland and England were fully united in 1707.

▲ For England!

England became very powerful in the Middle Ages. It fought many wars against its neighbours. This fierce battle took place at Agincourt, in France, in 1415. It was a victory for Henry V (Henry the Fifth) of England.

▲ Welsh uprising

The Welsh battled with the English, too, but were conquered in 1283. In 1400, the Welsh rose up against English rule, under a leader called Owain Glyndwr. The English were back in control by 1413 and the two countries were united in 1542.

◄ Irish freedom

England tried to rule Ireland for centuries, and it did become part of the United Kingdom from 1801. In 1916, there was an uprising in Dublin against British rule. The country won independence after 1922, but the North remained within the United Kingdom.

Byzantine Empire

In AD324, the Romans decided to make the city of Byzantium, in the east of their empire, every bit as grand as Rome. Byzantium was renamed Constantinople. The city survived long after Rome itself had fallen, ruling large areas of southern Europe and western Asia. In 1453, it was captured by the Turks, who called it Istanbul.

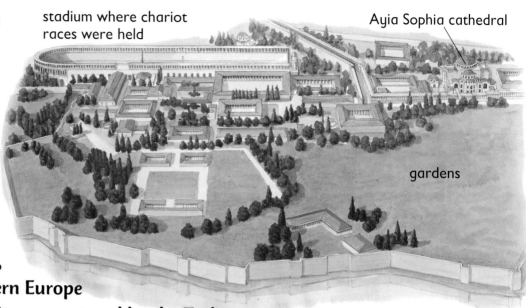

stadium where chariot races were held

Ayia Sophia cathedral

gardens

Wow!

Theodora was the daughter of a circus bear-tamer. She married the emperor Justinian in AD525, and became the most powerful woman in the world.

▲ Man of law

The emperor Justinian lived from about AD482 to AD565. Under his rule the Byzantines recaptured many lands of the old Roman Empire. He was a great law-maker.

▲ Constantinople

The city was a rich seaport with high walls. It had markets, workshops, gardens and a beautiful cathedral. The people who lived there were mostly Greeks.

▼ Holy wisdom

The city of Constantinople was an important centre of the Christian faith. It was full of churches and monasteries. The great cathedral, Ayia Sophia (meaning 'holy wisdom'), can still be visited today.

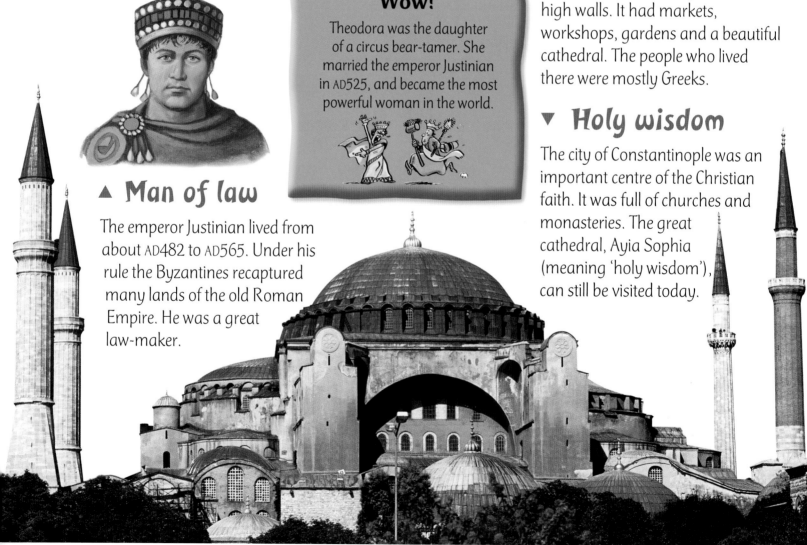

Canada

The first Canadians were hunters.
They may have crossed into Canada from Asia over 30,000 years ago. After about 3000BC, new people came from Asia to settle the frozen north, hunting polar bears and seals. Their descendants (family) are called Inuits.

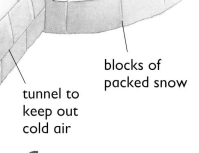

animal skins and fur to help keep the ice house warm inside

► Arctic survival

The Inuit built houses of stone and turf to keep out the bitter cold of winter. On hunting trips they made shelters out of ice blocks. These were surprisingly cosy.

blocks of packed snow

tunnel to keep out cold air

◄ European Canada

French and British explorers and settlers moved into Canada in the 1500s and 1600s, trading in fish and furs. In 1534, Jacques Cartier became the first European to explore the St Lawrence River.

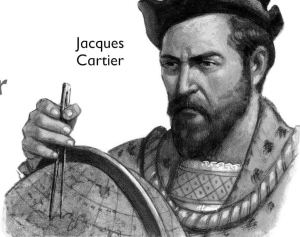

Jacques Cartier

▲ Mohawk warrior

The Mohawk people settled in southeast Canada and around the St Lawrence River. They lived in wooden houses and grew beans, maize, squash and tobacco.

◄ Canadian Pacific Railway

In 1885, a new railway was opened. It linked the eastern city of Montreal with Canada's Pacific coast. More and more Europeans travelled westwards and settled the land.

Castles

A castle was a kind of fortress home for kings, queens, lords and ladies. It had high towers and massive walls to keep out the enemy. Soldiers guarded the castle and controlled the surrounding countryside.

▶ The first castles

The first castles looked like this. They had a wooden tower, called a bailey, on top of a high mound of earth, called a motte. They were built by the Normans over 1,000 years ago.

motte-and-bailey castle

▲ Knock it down!

This giant catapult was called a trebuchet. It hurled rocks at castle walls in order to knock them down.

◀ Stronger and stronger

By 700 years ago, castles were being built with more and more round towers and walls. Around them were ditches filled with water, called moats. The walls of this castle, built at Conwy in Wales, went right around the town as well.

▶ Digging underneath

Enemy soldiers would surround a castle and cut off its supplies. This was called a siege, and it could go on for months, or even years. Sometimes the enemy tunnelled underneath the castle walls to make them fall down.

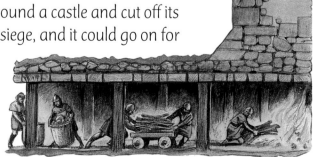

Word box

catapult
a weapon of war, designed to fire rocks and boulders

fortress
a building or town that has been specially built to protect it from attack

Celts

The ancient Celts were farmers and iron workers. Their homeland was in central and western Europe. Between about 700BC and 300BC, Celtic warriors swarmed across Europe, bringing their languages and ways of life to many regions. Celtic peoples included the Gauls of northern Italy and France, the Gaels of Ireland and the Britons of Great Britain.

▲ Charioteers

A Celtic charioteer practises his skills. His job was to drive a fully-armed warrior into the thick of battle at high speed.

◄ Furious fighters

Celtic tribes often fought against each other. Many also went to war with the Romans, Greeks and Germans. Their warriors were armed with iron swords, daggers, spears and long shields.

◄ Mirror, mirror

This beautiful bronze hand mirror was used by Celts in southern Britain over 2,000 years ago. The Celts also loved wearing gold jewellery. The Romans complained that they liked showing off too much!

▼ The hill fort

Maiden Castle, in southern Britain, was the chief town of a Celtic tribe. It was on a high hilltop, defended by fences and steep ditches. It was attacked and captured by the Romans after they invaded Britain in AD43.

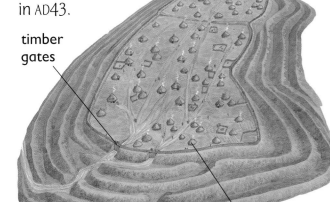

timber gates

wooden houses

► Later Celts

The Celts worshipped various gods and spirits, but during the AD300s and AD400s they turned to Christianity. Ireland became a centre of the faith and produced beautiful religious books, stone crosses and silver work.

China: beginnings

Find out more:
China: Empire and Republic ▶

The ancient Chinese believed that they lived at the centre of the world. They built great cities and canals and learned how to make beautiful silk, paper and pottery. Many of the world's most useful things were invented long ago in China.

meeting house in centre of village

hole in roof to let out smoke

thatched roof

wooden wall plastered with mud

supporting poles

▼ Ghostly army

By 221BC, China was a united empire. The first emperor (Qin Shi Huangdi, pictured left), was a powerful man. Only one thing scared him – death. Just before he died, he arranged for an army of life-sized terracotta (clay) soldiers to stand guard around his tomb.

◀ First farmers

This is what a northern Chinese village would have looked like over 5,000 years ago. The farmers living there grew millet and kept pigs and dogs. They made pottery. Rice was grown in central and southern China.

▶ The Great Wall

The first emperor sent hundreds of thousands of workers north to build a great wall. It was meant to stop fierce tribes from invading China. Work on the wall carried on for hundreds of years. When it was finished, it measured over 6,000 kilometres in length.

China: Empire and Republic

Find out more:
China: beginnings ◄

For 2,000 years the Chinese Empire grew bigger and bigger. Its merchants traded with India, the Middle East and distant Europe. The Empire survived wars and invasions until it came to an end in 1911, when it became a republic.

◄ A golden age

During the period AD618 to AD907, China became extremely wealthy. It made the first ever printed books and produced the world's finest pottery, such as this horse figurine.

► Forbidden City

Twenty-four emperors made their homes in this splendid palace at Beijing, between 1423 and 1911. It included 800 separate buildings. Ordinary people were never allowed inside its high red walls, so it became known as 'the Forbidden City'.

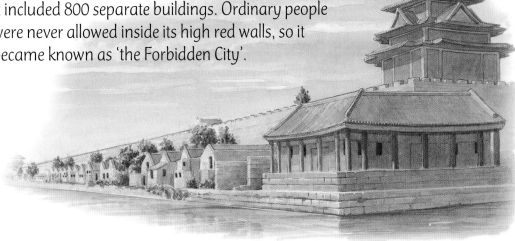

▲ Silk robes

The emperors of China ruled over a glittering court. They wore robes of silk, such as this one decorated with dragons.

► Power to the people

After 1911, there were many wars. The Japanese invaded China during the 1930s. Different political groups fought each other, too. The Communists, led by Mao Zedong, aimed to give power to poor working people. They ruled China after 1949.

Make a Chinese fan

1. Take a sheet of A4 paper.
2. Use colour felt-tip pens to make a Chinese dragon design.
3. Fold the paper into pleats.
4. Staple the bottom end of the fan together.

Cities of ancient times

Find out more:
Cities of modern times ▶
Housing and shelter ▶

When people lived by hunting, they had to follow herds of wild animals in order to survive. Only when they began farming could people settle down in one place, with a sure supply of food. Villages grew into towns and cities where people traded goods. The world's first towns were built in western Asia about 10,000 years ago.

▲ A town with no streets

Çatal Hüyük was built by farmers in about 7000BC, beside a river in Turkey. Its houses were made of mud bricks and flat roofs. They were all joined up, with no streets in between.

▲ Walls and gates

The city of Babylon was built beside the river Euphrates, Iraq, about 3,800 years ago. It was protected by massive walls. Nine gates led into the city. The Ishtar Gate was covered with blue tiles, decorated with bulls and dragons. Through it, a paved highway led to temples and royal palaces.

▼ Gardens of Babylon

A thousand years after it was built, Babylon was still a great city. It was famous for its beautiful terraces and gardens, made for a queen called Seramis.

How many people?

See how the number of people in each ancient city grew over time:

3000BC	Uruk (Iraq)	50,000
2200BC	Ur (Iraq)	250,000
600BC	Babylon (Iraq)	350,000
200BC	Patna (India)	500,000
100BC	Rome (Italy)	1,100,000

Cities of modern times

Find out more:
Cities of ancient times ◀
Housing and shelter ▶

In the 1800s, country people began to pour into the cities around the world to work in new factories and offices. Some cities now housed as many as four million people. Numbers doubled and doubled again in the 1900s. Today, one in three people in the world lives in a town or a city.

◀ City of London

London, the capital of the United Kingdom, became the world's biggest city in the 1880s. Roads, railways and houses soon swallowed up farmland around the city. Factory and household smoke made cities dirty places to live.

How many people?
See how the number of people in each modern city has grown:

AD900	Angkor (Cambodia)	1,000,000
1279	Hangzhou (China)	1,500,000
1890	New York City (USA)	1,500,000
1939	London (England)	8,600,000
1990	Tokyo-Yokohama (Japan)	27,200,000

▲ The Eiffel Tower

This 300-metre-high tower was put up in Paris, France, in 1889, to mark a big exhibition. At that time it was the world's highest building.

▶ Reach for the sky

During the 1890s, skyscrapers were built in the centres of New York City and Chicago. They took up very little space at ground level. They were made possible by new ways of building and by the invention of the lift. These buildings are the Petronas Towers in Kuala Lumpur, Malaysia.

▲ Under the ground

Cities built underground railways from the 1860s onwards. The Moscow Metro, built in the 1930s, has very grand stations, like this one.

Clothes

Find out more:
Ancient Roman life ◀ French Revolution and after ▶
Middle Ages ▶ Vikings ▶

The first humans made simple clothes from animal skins, furs and plant fibres. By about 7000BC, people had learned to weave cloth on looms. Wool, linen and cotton were often used for keeping warm or staying cool. Different styles of clothes were worn around the world.

brooch to fix tunic to shoulder

tunic

shift

long dress, or *stola*

toga

thick cloak, or *palla*

▲ Viking dress

Viking women wore a shift with a long woollen tunic over the top. The men wore a knee-length tunic over trousers, with a cloak for warmth.

▲ Roman togas

In ancient Rome, important men wrapped themselves in a heavy white robe called a toga. Senators who passed the laws wore a toga with a purple stripe. Most women wore several layers of cloth.

▼ A true gentleman

This is how European men dressed in the 1700s. They wore long 'frock-coat' over a waistcoat, knee-length breeches and a three-cornered hat. Both men and women wore white wigs, over their own hair.

▲ In the Middle Ages

In Europe during the Middle Ages, most poor children wore simple clothes woven from home-made wool. Boys wore short tunics and girls long ones. Hoods and cloaks kept off the rain.

◀ Paris fashions

The French were famous for fashion as long ago as the Middle Ages. In the 1800s and 1900s, women all over Europe and North America searched magazines for the very latest Paris designs. These ones date from 1913.

Crusades

In 1075, Turkish Muslims captured the holy city of Jerusalem. In 1096, after the Muslims declared that pilgrims could no longer visit Jerusalem, Christian knights living in Europe began a series of religious wars called the Crusades. Most of these were fought against Muslims in the Near East, but others took place in Spain and Central Europe.

► Saladin

One Saracen leader was admired and respected even by his enemies. His name was Saladin, or Saleh-ed-din Yussuf, and he lived from 1137 to 1193.

► Sword on sword

Terrible wars were fought in the Near East until 1291. The Christian knights wore heavy armour, even in the heat of the desert. Their Muslim enemies were armed with steel swords, round shields and bows and arrows. The Europeans called them 'Saracens'.

Word box

Crusades
'wars of the Cross', the Cross being the badge of the Christian knights

Near East
the lands of southwest Asia, today occupied by Turkey, Syria, Lebanon, Israel and the Palestinian Territories

Disasters

In the past, life was much less certain.
If the harvest was bad, everyone went hungry.
People suffered, as we do today, from floods,
fires, volcanoes and earthquakes, but in those
days they had no fire engines or
rescue teams. There was little
understanding of disease and
no modern medicine.

▲ The plague

Between 1347 and 1351, a terrible illness
called the Black Death raged across Asia
and Europe. It was passed on to humans
by rat fleas and killed about 75 million
people. This deadly disease, or plague,
returned again and again. It killed tens
of thousands of people in London in 1665.

▲ Great Fire of London

When houses were mostly built of wood, there was a great
risk from fire. In 1666, a fire at a London bakery spread
across the city, destroying over 13,000 homes.

Wow!

In AD472, so many ashes erupted
out of the volcano Vesuvius that
they were carried as far away
as Turkey!

► Volcano disaster!

Almost 2,000 years ago, the entire
Roman town of Pompeii was buried
under hot ashes when the volcano
Vesuvius erupted in AD79. Since then,
it has erupted several more
times, with equal force.

Empires and colonies

Find out more:
Britain and Ireland ◄
Spain and Portugal ►

In the 1500s and 1600s, the Europeans discovered new lands in Africa, Asia and the Americas. They wanted to take away the riches of these countries and rule the people who lived there. By the 1800s and early 1900s, Britain, France, Germany, the Netherlands, Belgium, Portugal and Spain controlled vast empires.

▲ Queen and Empress

During the reign of Queen Victoria, from 1837 to 1901, Britain ruled the world's largest ever empire. It stretched from Canada to India and from Africa to Australia and the South Pacific.

▼ Cruelty in the Caribbean

Spain, Britain and France ruled the Caribbean islands. They grew sugar cane there, using slaves from Africa. The slaves were treated with great cruelty. Slavery continued in the Caribbean until the 1830s.

▲ Bolívar of Bolivia

Spain ruled much of South America. By the 1800s, many colonists (settlers) wanted to break away from the old country. In 1811, a soldier called Simón Bolívar began to fight for the freedom of Venezuela, Colombia, Ecuador, Peru and Bolivia.

► Freedom for India

By the 1900s, nations were demanding their freedom. Sometimes they went to war against their colonial rulers. The great Indian leader, Mohandas K. Gandhi, believed in peaceful protests. The British left India in 1947.

Explorers at sea

Find out more:
Australia ◄ Explorers on land ►
New Zealand and the Pacific ► Vikings ►

In the days of sailing ships, sea voyages could last many years. Sailors had to find their way across the oceans, battle with storms and survive shipwrecks. When they did land on unknown shores, they risked being attacked by the local people.

▲ Leif the Lucky

The Vikings were great seafarers. Their ships, called longships, reached Iceland and Greenland. In 1000, a sailor called Leif 'the Lucky' Eriksson reached North America.

▲ A vast fleet

Between 1405 and 1433, the Chinese admiral Zheng He made seven voyages, exploring the Indian Ocean. On his first voyage there were 62 big boats called junks, 225 small boats and 27,000 men!

► Captain Cook

James Cook was an English sea captain who was a brilliant navigator (explorer). In the 1760s and 1770s, he explored the Pacific Ocean and the coasts of New Zealand and Australia.

► Great voyages

This map shows some of the great voyages of exploration. Look at the map key to find out which explorer sailed which route.

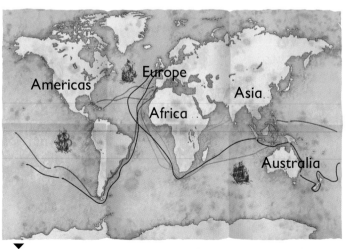

Americas
Europe
Africa
Asia
Australia

Map key

Red: Christopher Columbus, 1492
Yellow: Vasco da Gama, 1497–98
Green: Magellan, 1519–22
Purple: James Cook, 1768–71

Explorers on land

Find out more:
Explorers at sea ◄

Today, every place on Earth has been mapped.
Only 200 years ago, many maps included blank areas,
showing unknown lands. Travel was slow and often
dangerous, but many brave men and women set out
to explore the world.

▼ Tireless traveller

Ibn Batutah came from Tangiers in
North Africa. He travelled from
1325 to 1354, reaching
the Middle East,
India, China and
Southeast Asia.
He also journeyed
south across the
Sahara Desert to
the city of Timbuktu.

▼ Africa explored

From the 1850s, a Scottish explorer
called David Livingstone made
many journeys across Africa.
By 1869 he was believed lost, so
another British explorer, Henry
Morton Stanley, set out to look for
him. He found Livingstone in 1871.

Word scramble

Can you unscramble these
words to find destinations
for explorers?

a. ELOP THRON
b. EVIRR NOAMAZ
c. AHARAS DETRES
d. WEN AGUINE

answers
a. North Pole b. river Amazon
c. Sahara Desert d. New Guinea

▼ To the South Pole

Howling winds and bitter cold failed
to stop explorer Roald Amundsen,
a Norwegian, from crossing icy
Antarctica to
reach the South
Pole in 1911.

Roald
Amundsen

◄ Jungle journeys

From 1799 to 1804, Alexander
von Humboldt, from Germany,
and Aimé Bonpland, from France,
survived in the steamy rainforests
of South America. They came
across electric eels and alligators
and brought back 12,000
samples of plants.

Alexander
von
Humboldt

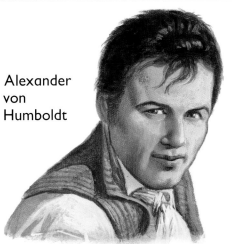

Farming

Long ago, people gathered wild plants and ate roots, leaves and seeds. They found that if they planted some of the seeds each year, they could grow crops for food. They also learned to tame wild animals, such as goats and sheep. Farming began in the Middle East, about 10,000 years ago.

steam-powered tractor, late 1800s

▲ The first farmers

By choosing only the best seed each year, farmers turned wild grasses into useful grain crops such as wheat or barley. They harvested them with tools made of stone, wood and bone.

▲ Nice rice!

Farming started in different parts of the world at different times. Rice was grown in China 7,000 years ago. It was often sown in flooded fields like these ones. Rice became the most important crop in Asia.

▼ Sowing seed

In Europe during the Middle Ages, horses or oxen were used to plough the soil and prepare it for sowing. Seed was scattered by hand.

▲ Soil-buster

Steam power began to be used to drive farm machinery in the 1800s. In the 1900s, the first petrol-driven tractors were made.

Word box

crops
plants that can be grown for food, such as rice or wheat, or for making cloth, such as cotton

tame
make a wild animal used to living and working with people

Food

Until explorers reached the Americas in the 1500s, no Europeans had ever seen potatoes or tomatoes. For thousands of years, people only ate food that was grown locally. By the 1800s, foods were traded right around the world. Australians were drinking tea from China and Europeans were eating beef from Argentina.

tomatoes

chillies

▲▼ American foods

Foods first eaten in ancient Central and South America include tomatoes, avocado pears, chillies, squashes, potatoes and cocoa. Today they are enjoyed everywhere in the world.

avocado pear

Wow!

When Vesuvius blew its top in AD79, it buried the whole town of Herculaneum in boiling mud. It preserved the food laid out for lunch for hundreds of years.

▼ Keeping it sweet

In ancient Egypt, Greece and Rome there was no sugar made from cane. Instead, cakes and puddings were sweetened with honey. Honey bees were kept on farms.

► A castle banquet

During the Middle Ages in Europe, poor people went hungry while splendid banquets were held by lords and ladies. They dined off boar's head or swan meat, ate the finest white bread and drank wine.

▲ Roman take-away

Street stalls and bars sold food and snacks in Roman towns and cities. People ate pies and sausages on their way to the Colosseum, the circular theatre where they watched fights between gladiators.

France

After the Romans left Gaul (France), it was invaded by the Franks, who came from Germany. So the country became known as France. During the Middle Ages, France became one of the most powerful countries in Europe, famous for its arts and learning and the fine manners of its knights and ladies.

▲ Charlemagne

This great king of the Franks lived from AD747 to AD814. He ruled over an empire that stretched all the way from the borders of Spain to central Europe. Charlemagne means 'Charles the Great'.

▲ The Sun King

Louis XIV (Louis the Fourteenth) was king of France from 1643 to 1715. He ruled over a glittering court and was very powerful. He was nicknamed the 'Sun King'.

◄ Notre Dame

In 1163, workers began to build an impressive cathedral beside the river Seine, in Paris. It was called Notre Dame, which means 'Our Lady'.

▲ Joan of Arc

During the Middle Ages, France was forever at war with England. In the 1420s, a girl called Joan of Arc claimed that she heard voices from God, saying that the English soldiers must be thrown out of France. She fought with the French army until she was captured and burnt alive by the English.

Word box

cathedral
an important church building, headed by a bishop or an archbishop

court
the lords, ladies and officials at a royal palace

French Revolution and after

Find out more:
France ◀

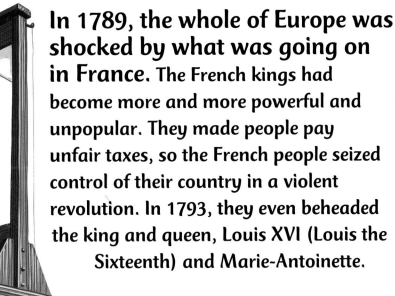

In 1789, the whole of Europe was shocked by what was going on in France. The French kings had become more and more powerful and unpopular. They made people pay unfair taxes, so the French people seized control of their country in a violent revolution. In 1793, they even beheaded the king and queen, Louis XVI (Louis the Sixteenth) and Marie-Antoinette.

◀ 'Long live the emperor!'

Napoleon Bonaparte lived from 1761 to 1821. He was a brilliant soldier who fought in the Revolution, and later made himself emperor of France. He won great battles all over Europe and made new laws.

▲ Days of terror

This dreadful machine was called the guillotine. It was designed for cutting off people's heads. During the Revolution, rich lords and ladies were sent to the guillotine. Then the rebels began to quarrel amongst themselves and sent each other to be killed instead.

▲ Waterloo

The cannons crash, soldiers yell and horses neigh. In 1815, the French and their emperor, Napoleon, were finally defeated at Waterloo, in Belgium, by the British and Prussian armies.

Word scramble

In the 1800s, Napoleon's armies fought against the following countries. Can you unscramble their names?

a. ISURATA
b. ASSURI
c. PASSIRU
d. REGAT NIBITAR

answers
a. Austria b. Russia c. Prussia d. Great Britain

◀ Naughty nineties

In the 1890s, Paris was famous for the wild lives led by its artists, poets, dancers and performers. A high-kicking dance called the cancan was all the rage.

Germany

GERMANY UNITES 1815–1871

SWEDEN
DENMARK
UNITED KINGDOM
GERMANY
RUSSIA
AUSTRIA
FRANCE
HUNGARY
ITALY

- ▨ German Confederation 1815
- ▨ Prussia 1866
- ▨ German Empire 1871

For centuries, Germany was made up of hundreds of different states and nations. Some of them were part of the Holy Roman Empire. During the 1800s, they began to group together and, by 1871, a united German Empire had been formed.

▲ Prussian power

The German kingdom of Prussia was founded in 1701. In 1756, it fought against Austria, starting the Seven Years' War. By the 1800s, Prussia was the most powerful German nation.

▼ Music-makers

In the 1700s and 1800s, Germany became a centre of the arts. Some of the world's greatest musicians lived here at this time, including Ludwig van Beethoven. Amongst his many masterpieces, he wrote nine symphonies, an opera, *Fidelio*, and a religious work called a Mass.

◀ Fairy-tale palace

This fantastic castle was built for King Ludwig II. He ruled the southern kingdom of Bavaria from 1864 until 1886, when he was declared mad.

Wow!
The world's tallest cathedral spire is to be seen in Ulm, Germany. It soars to a height of over 160 metres.

▼ One country

King Wilhelm I of Prussia was made emperor of all Germany in 1871. Berlin became the capital city of the united country. At this time many new factories, steelworks and mines were being built in Germany.

Holland and Belgium

Find out more:
Art in history ◄ Farming ◄
Middle Ages ►

Belgium and the Netherlands (meaning 'lowlands') border the North Sea. Part of the Netherlands is called Holland, and many people use the word 'Netherlands' instead of Holland. The people of this region fought many European wars, but their greatest enemy has always been the sea, which has flooded this coast for thousands of years.

◄ Tulip madness!

In the 1600s, Holland became a rich nation that traded around the world. At this time, there was a huge craze amongst merchants for buying and selling tulip bulbs. Tulips and other flowers are still traded today.

◄ Why windmills?

The countryside in Holland is dotted with old windmills. For hundreds of years, wind power was used to pump water out of the soggy farmland.

▲ Old Antwerp

Antwerp is an old Belgian port on the river Scheldt. In the Middle Ages it was an important centre for the cloth trade. This statue is of the painter Peter Paul Rubens, who made the city his home in 1608.

What did they do?

Can you find out? Match these famous Lowlanders with the part they played in history:

1. Jan van Eyck
2. Abel Janszoon Tasman
3. Erasmus of Rotterdam
4. Leopold I
5. William of Orange

a. The first king of independent Belgium
b. A great scholar
c. A Dutch ruler who became king of England
d. A famous painter of the Middle Ages
e. An explorer of the 1600s

1d 2e 3b 4a 5c
answers

Wow!

More than 40 percent of Dutch land used to be under the waves! Over the years it has been sealed off by sea walls and then drained.

▲ The lacemaker

Many great Dutch painters lived in the 1600s. This picture by Jan Vermeer shows a lacemaker. Holland and Belgium were famous for their fine lace.

Holy Roman Empire

The Holy Roman Empire was an alliance of many small European states and nations. It followed on from the empire of Charlemagne. The states had their own rulers, but they recognized the Holy Roman emperor as their leader. The Empire lasted from AD962 to 1806 and was at its height during the Middle Ages.

LAND OF THE EMPERORS IN THE MIDDLE AGES

Lowlands Saxony

GERMANY

Franconia   BOHEMIA

Austria

BURGUNDY Bavaria

LOMBARDY

SICILY

► The Empire

The Holy Roman Empire was a group of lands that at various times included the Netherlands, Austria, much of Germany, central Europe and Italy.

▲ Red Beard

Frederick I, who became emperor in 1152, belonged to a powerful German family called Hohenstaufen. He was nicknamed Barbarossa, which means 'red beard'. He was drowned while on a Crusade in 1190.

► A two-headed eagle

The badge of the Holy Roman Empire was a two-headed eagle. After 1452, the Empire was ruled by an Austrian family called the Habsburgs. They also became rulers of Spain.

◄ Castle of wonders

Castel del Monte was built in about 1240 in southern Italy. It was one of the many strong castles built for the emperor Frederick II, who was Barbarossa's grandson. He was nicknamed 'Wonder of the World'.

Housing and shelter

Find out more:
Ancient Roman life ◄ Cities of ancient times ◄
Cities of modern times ◄ Stone Age ►

Human beings have always needed shelter and shade. They have learned to make homes from whatever materials are available. Tents could be sewn from animal skins or cloth. Huts could be made from turf, branches, leaves or bamboo canes. Houses have been built from timber, clay or stone. Over the ages, people learned how to make bricks, concrete, steel girders and glass windows.

◄ Cave-dwellers

During the Stone Age, caves offered families shelter and protection from wild animals. However, they were often damp, dark and draughty.

▲ Brick and slate

Big cities were built in Britain in the 1800s, with inexpensive housing for factory workers. Bricks and slates for the roofs could be carried from far away by canals or railways.

▼ Timber frame

In the Middle Ages, most houses were built with timber frames. These made criss-cross patterns on the walls, as seen on this German house.

heated swimming pool

courtyard

dining room

walled garden

kitchen

▲ A Roman home

Roman villas were built with tiled roofs and central courtyards. Many had beautiful gardens decorated with statues.

Ice ages

Between about a million and ten thousand years ago, the Earth went through several periods when it was bitterly cold. Huge sheets of ice spread out from the Poles. During these ice ages, lands that now have a mild climate were deep in snow and their rivers were frozen solid.

Word box

climate
the kind of weather experienced in one place over a long period of time

Poles
the most northerly and southerly points on Earth

upright man, about 1.6 million years ago

Neanderthal man, about 200,000 to 30,000 years ago

modern man, about 40,000 years ago to present day

▲ Ice age people

Various types of human being lived through the ice ages and learned how to survive the cold. By the end of the ice ages, only modern man, our direct ancestor (relative from a long time ago), lived on Earth.

▲ Mammoth hunters

Big hairy elephants called woolly mammoths and woolly rhinoceroses roamed the land during the ice ages. People hunted them with weapons made of wood and stone.

Incas

When Spanish explorers reached South America in the 1500s they heard rumours of a fabulous land rich in gold. In fact, there had been splendid civilizations in the Andes Mountains and along the Pacific coast for thousands of years. The latest great empire was that of the Incas. It lasted from about 1100 to 1532, when it was conquered by the Spanish.

Wow!

The Temple of the Sun in Cuzco had a garden in which everything, including model plants and animals, was made of solid silver and gold.

▲ Nazca puzzles

The Nazca civilization was one of many before the Incas. It lasted from about 200BC to AD750. Its people scraped patterns on the desert floor. These may have shown routes for religious processions. Some, like this hummingbird, were animal shaped.

▲ Road-runner

Messengers like this one carried the emperor's orders through the Inca Empire. He carries a *quipu*, or bunch of cords. These were knotted as a way of remembering numbers or other information.

▼ The Inca Empire

The Inca Empire was called Tawantisuyu, which means 'the Four Quarters'. It was centred on Peru and also took in large areas of Ecuador, Chile and Bolivia. It stretched 3,600 kilometres from north to south.

◀ Machu Picchu

The remains of this Inca town can be found high in the mountain peaks of Peru. The Incas were great builders, farmers and craftworkers.

India

Rich cloth, beautiful stone carvings, paintings and wonderful poetry were produced in ancient India. Several great empires grew up there. The Maurya Empire was at its height around 250BC and Gupta rule in about AD350. Hinduism and Buddhism also grew and spread during this period.

◄ Mughal Empire

Northern India was under Muslim rule from 1211. In 1526, the Mughal Empire was founded. This is Emperor Shah Jahan, who lived from 1592 to 1666.

▼ Taj Mahal

Shah Jahan had this marble monument built by the river Yamuna in honour of his wife, Mumtaz Mahal, who died in 1631. It was decorated with precious stones.

▲ Holy caves

There is a cave temple on Elephanta Island near Mumbai (Bombay) that is more than 1,200 years old. The temple has wonderful carvings of Hindu gods, such as Shiva.

◄ Indian dance

Indian dance has a history dating back thousands of years. It is said that the Hindu god, Shiva, set the world spinning by his dancing.

Indus Valley

Find out more:
Cities of ancient times ◀ Farming ◀
▶ Money and trade

The Indus River flows through Pakistan to the Arabian Sea. Between about 2500BC and 1750BC, a great civilization grew up in the Indus Valley. The people living there grew cotton and grain. They worked in metal and produced pottery, cloth and jewellery, trading with the peoples of western Asia.

◀ Mystery man

This stone head was made in Mohenjo-daro in about 2100BC. Whose face is it? Nobody really knows for certain. It might belong to a god, a king or a priest.

▼ How they lived

Pottery models, such as this one showing a two-wheeled cart drawn by bullocks, show us how people used to live in Harappa.

▲ Mohenjo-daro

The two greatest cities of the Indus Valley were Harappa and Mohenjo-daro. They had streets and proper drains, and houses built of bricks.

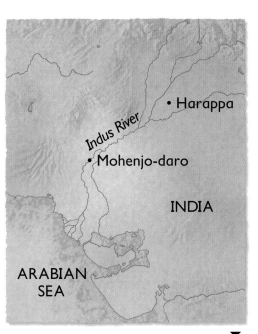

▲ Trade marks

Stone seals were used by the merchants of Mohenjo-daro to mark bundles of trade goods. Many show animals or a name.

◀ The great river

Flooding from the Indus River left behind rich soil for farming. The civilization that grew up along the riverbanks stretched into India.

Make a stone seal

1. Ask an adult to help you. Take a block of modelling clay. Using a knife, cut a design based on your favourite animal.
2. Write your name along the top, and allow clay to harden.
3. Press the top into a saucer of paint or ink, then press onto a piece of paper or card.

Industrial Revolution

Find out more

Cities of modern times ◄ Victorian Britain

The age of factories and machines began in Europe and North America in the 1700s and 1800s. It is called the Industrial Revolution, a term used to describe the changes brought about when people used steam to make goods. At first, the people who worked in the new factories had to work long hours for little pay.

▼ Steam power

The factory age was possible because of the invention of the steam engine. This engine was made in the 1700s, by an inventor called Thomas Newcomen.

▼ Cities and smoke

During the Industrial Revolution, cities grew and spread across Europe. This is a typical British city scene. It had street after street of small red-brick houses and tall chimneys belching out smoke.

Word box

factory
a building where machines are used to make goods on a large scale

steam engine
any machine whose movement is powered by the force of steam (which is made when water boils)

Can you imagine a world without wheels, without petrol engines, without medicines? For thousands of years clever people have invented machines and gadgets. Many of these have made our lives easier, safer or more healthy.

▲ The wheel

The wheel is one of the most important things ever invented. Flat wheels were probably first used by potters, to turn their clay into round pots. By about 3500BC, upright wheels were being used for transport on chariots or wagons in the Middle East.

▼ North, south, east, west

Compasses use magnetism to show which direction to travel in — north, south, east or west. The first compasses were made in China over 2,300 years ago. At first, they looked like metal spoons with handles that pointed south. Later, steel needles were floated in bowls of water.

Hooke's microscope

◀ Magnification

Microscopes make even the tiniest objects look big. The first ones were made in the Netherlands in about 1590. This one was made in England in 1665, by a scientist called Robert Hooke. It was the first one to look like a modern microscope. Hooke used it to study the structure of chemicals and plants.

▶ Thomas Edison

An American called Thomas Edison invented the electric light bulb in 1879. He had already invented the phonograph, which recorded sound and played it back again.

Iron Age

Find out more:
African kingdoms ◄ Ancient Roman Empire ◄ Celts ◄
China: beginnings ◄

Learning how to work iron was one of the most important discoveries ever made by human beings. Iron could now be used to make much stronger weapons and tools than had been possible before. It was being smelted by west Asian peoples, such as the Hittites, about 4,000 years ago. Iron-working skills soon spread to Europe, North Africa and other parts of Asia.

Word box

bellows
machines designed to puff air at glowing coals in a furnace, to make them hotter

ploughshare
the blade on a plough that turns over the soil

smelting
heating rock so that the metal it contains is melted and taken out

◄ Chinese plough

The ancient Chinese were very skilled iron workers. They made the first iron ploughshares in the world, over 2,500 years ago, to a design still in use today. They also invented cast iron, over 2,300 years ago.

◄ Iron swords

Iron was a deadly metal when used for making weapons. This short Roman sword was called a *gladius*. It was used by Roman armies to cut down their enemies.

◄ Iron in Africa

These men are using bellows to fan an iron-smelting furnace in Africa. Iron was being used south of the Sahara Desert by about 500BC, and had reached southern Africa by 200BC.

bellows forced air through the clay pipes to make the fire hotter

firewood for burning

furnace

the fire in the furnace needed to be extremely hot to melt the metal

bellows

clay pipes

Italy

During the Middle Ages, Italy was split up into small states. Some of them were ruled by other nations, others were independent republics. The great city of Rome was the centre of the Catholic Church and the home of its leader, the Pope. It was not until the 1800s that the different regions of Italy began to join together as a single nation.

▲ Leaning tower

This bell tower in the city of Pisa was built in 1170. Standing on sandy soil it soon started to tilt – and is still leaning over at an angle today.

▼ Popes of Rome

During the Middle Ages, the pope was the most powerful man in Europe. He wore a special crown called a tiara.

▲ The Red Shirts

In the 1860s, Giuseppe Garibaldi and his followers, the 'Red Shirts', fought for a united Italy. By 1871, Italy had become one nation again.

Make your own carnival mask

1. Ask an adult to help you. Cut a card mask to fit your face.

2. Paint it in gold or silver paint and decorate it with felt-tip pens.

3. Pierce two holes level with your ears. Tie string through the holes to attach the mask to your face.

▲ Venetian Carnival

The winter festival of Carnival has been held in Venice since the Middle Ages. People still wear masks and fancy costumes to the Carnival today.

Japan and Korea

Farmers have been growing rice on the lands around the Sea of Japan for over 2,000 years. Over the centuries, the islands of Japan were ruled by emperors and warriors, while powerful kings ruled over Korea. Beautiful buildings, pottery, paintings, prints, poetry and plays were all produced in this part of Asia.

◄ Knights of the East

The samurai were Japanese knights. They held great power between the 1100s and 1600s. The samurai fought for local lords, armed with sharp swords, bows and arrows, and later with guns.

▼ Tea time

In the 1400s, Buddhist monks in Japan made tea according to a long and complicated ritual. This became known as *chanoyu*, a tea-drinking ceremony which still takes place in Japan today. It aims to show off polite manners, friendship and beauty and takes several hours.

▲ Fine writing

In Korea, as in China, calligraphy (fine handwriting) is very much admired. Chinese, Western and Korean forms of writing may be seen in Korea. The Korean script is called *hangeul* and it dates back as far as the 1400s.

▲ Japanese castles

During the 1500s, Japanese lords built towering castles. They were very strong, being made of timber, earth and stone.

Wow!

Japan's royal family is the oldest in the world. It has ruled the country for over 2,000 years.

Kings and queens

Find out more:
Castles ◄ Empires and colonies ◄ Middle Ages ►
Russia ►

Most countries used to be ruled by kings and queens, who were often very powerful. Sometimes, they claimed to rule by the will of God. When they died, their children often ruled the country after them. Today, some countries are still ruled by kings and queens, but they have less power than in the Middle Ages.

Queen Elizabeth I

▲ Crown jewels

Kings and queens have always owned crowns with sparkling jewels, as an emblem (badge) of their royal power. Other emblems were held in the ruler's hands. They included big swords, rods called sceptres and globes called orbs.

▲ Rulers no more

In 1917, many Russians decided that they did not want to be ruled by their tsar (emperor) any longer. In the revolution that followed, Nicholas II and his whole family were killed.

◄ Women in power

In certain countries, only men were allowed to rule. But some of the world's strongest rulers have been women. Queen Elizabeth I ruled England from 1558 to 1603. Nobody dared to argue with her!

◄ Royal palaces

Kings and queens often lived in splendid homes. Louis XIV (Louis the Fourteenth) had a huge palace built at the village of Versailles in France. Work began in 1661 and continued for a century (100 years).

Knights

In Europe, between about 1000 and 1500, horseback fighters that were heavily armed became the most important soldiers on the battlefield. They were called knights. Many knights were well rewarded with land and money. They went on to become powerful lords.

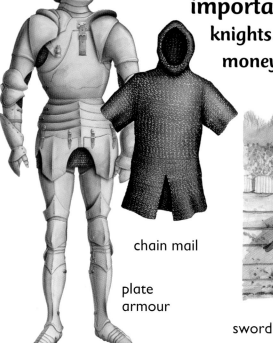

chain mail

plate armour

▲ Shining armour

In the 1000s, knights wore armour made of small iron rings, called chain mail. Later, they wore plates of metal joined together to cover the whole body. This was plate armour.

sword

mace

◄ Heavy weapons

Knights fought with long spears called lances, and with axes, swords and clubs called maces.

◄ Take that!

Knights liked to take part in mock battles called tournaments, or jousts, to show off their fighting skills. They wore fancy armour and helmets.

▲ Code of honour

Knights were expected to behave in an honourable way and to respect ladies. People loved to hear stories about chivalry, the noble manners of knights. In reality, many knights were brutal and selfish.

Design your own coat-of-arms

1. Ask an adult to help you. Cut out the shape of a shield from cardboard.
2. Design and colour in your own coat-of-arms. You might want to show things you are interested in, or base the design on your name – a loaf for Baker, say, or a pot for Potter. If your name is Green or Brown, you might want to use that when choosing colours.

▼ Coats-of-arms

It was often hard to tell which knight was which when they were dressed in full armour. So the knights decorated their shields with their family badges, called coats-of-arms.

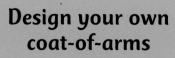

Medicine

Find out more:
Disasters ◄ Inventions ◄ Science ►

Doctors have been treating ill people for thousands of years, but with much less knowledge than doctors today. Some of them discovered useful plants for medicines, but many of the potions they mixed up did not help their patients at all. Great advances in medical knowledge came in the 1600s, and by the 1800s and 1900s many lives were saved.

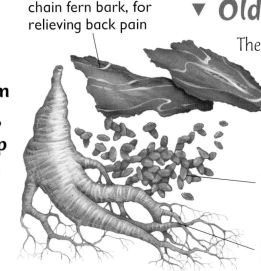

chain fern bark, for relieving back pain

▼ Old remedies

These Chinese medicines have been used for hundreds of years, and are still in use today.

wolfberry, for improving eyesight

ginseng, a root used to stimulate the body

▲ Florence Nightingale

In the 1850s, Florence Nightingale became famous for her care of wounded British soldiers. Horrified by poor standards in hospitals, she devoted her life to improving them and set up nurse training schools.

Lister's antiseptic spray

◄ Safe operations

In 1867, an English surgeon called Joseph Lister worked out how to kill germs during operations. He used a chemical spray such as this one and saved many lives.

▲ Understanding germs

A French scientist called Louis Pasteur, who lived from 1822 to 1895, helped us to understand how diseases are spread by germs or bacteria.

Middle Ages

Find out more:
Farming ◄ Religious buildings ►
Writing and printing ►

The period known in Europe as the Middle Ages lasted about 1,000 years. It was given that name because it lay in-between the ancient world and the modern age. The ancient world ended with the fall of the Roman Empire in AD476. The modern world began with the great voyages of exploration and scientific discoveries of the late 1400s and 1500s.

► Holy journeys

Christians who went on journeys to holy places were called pilgrims. Places of pilgrimage included Jerusalem, Rome and Canterbury in England. The pilgrims wore special badges to show which sites they had visited.

▲ A life of toil

In the 1100s, farm workers, called serfs, were forced to work for the local lord in exchange for some of the food they grew. They were not free to move away from their village.

▲ In praise of God

By the 1100s, most Europeans were Christians. Many cathedrals were built at this time, including this one at Chartres in France, built between 1195 and 1220.

Make a quill

During the Middle Ages, people used feathers called quills as pens. Next time you find a big feather, cut the end like a nib, dip it in some ink and use it to write your name.

► Fine words

Europeans did not learn how to print until the end of the Middle Ages. Before that, books had to be carefully copied out by hand. The words were beautifully written and decorated with pictures and patterns.

Money and trade

Find out more:
Ancient Egyptian life ◀ Ancient Greek cities ◀
Ancient Roman life ◀ Cities of ancient times ◀ Indus Valley ◀

The first traders swapped goods with one another. They might pay for a new basket with an axe, or pay for a sack of wheat with a goose. This was called bartering. It was not an accurate way to do business, so people began to use tokens such as metal coins instead. The value of each token was agreed by all the traders in the land.

▼ Metal coins

The oldest surviving coins were made in about 630BC for a Greek king called Gyges. He ruled Lydia, which is now in Turkey. The coins were made of electrum, a mixture of silver and gold.

a Roman coin, issued in 323BC and one of the first coins to be stamped with a ruler's head

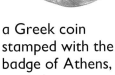
a Greek coin stamped with the badge of Athens, an owl

a solid gold English pound coin from the 1580s

▲ 'That will be six shells, please!'

All sorts of items were used as trading tokens at different times around the world. They included shells, beads, sharks' teeth, stones, blocks of salt or tea and metal rings. Coins were better because they were easy to carry and could not be broken.

▲ Long distance

Even in the ancient world, people traded over long distances. Egyptian ships, such as this one, carried goods from Crete, Arabia and East Africa to towns up and down the river Nile. The Romans bought spices from distant India and silk from China.

▼ Paper money

Paper money was first used in China over 1,000 years ago. This big press is printing banknotes in the 1800s.

Word box

press
a machine used for printing

trader
someone who takes part in the buying and selling of goods

Mongol Empire

Find out more:
China: Empire and Republic ◄ Middle Ages ◄

The rolling grasslands of eastern Europe and Asia are called steppes. In ancient times and during the Middle Ages, most of the people living there were nomads. They moved across the land with their herds and flocks, living in tents rather than towns. Some of the fiercest warriors came from the steppes of Mongolia.

► Riders of the steppes

Wild horses were first tamed on the grasslands. The peoples of the steppes were all expert riders.

▲ Into China

In 1211, the Mongols crossed the Great Wall and invaded northern China. Kublai Khan, grandson of Temujin, became the Chinese emperor in 1271.

▼ Samarkand

Timur the Lame, or Tamberlaine, ruled over Samarkand, a city in Uzbekistan. He lived from 1336 to 1405 and conquered lands stretching from Russia to India.

▼ Genghis Khan

Temujin lived from about 1162 to 1227. He became the ruler of the Mongols when he was just 13 and was soon leading his warriors into battle across Asia and eastern Europe. He became known as Genghis Khan, or 'mighty ruler'.

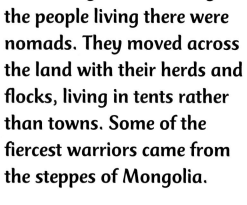

Word box

nomad
somebody who does not live in the same place all the time, but travels from one place to another

Music and dance

Stone Age people used to make pipes and whistles from bones and reeds. Drums too have been used for many thousands of years. People danced in honour of the gods or as a thanksgiving for spring or the harvest. Different kinds of music developed across the world at the same time.

▼ Flamenco!

Flamenco music is played in Spain. It includes strummed guitars, singing, shouting and clapping. Dancers strut, whirl and stamp. Flamenco probably began in the 1400s, when the Roma people (gypsies) first arrived in Europe. Over the years it has blended with Arab, Jewish and Spanish musical styles.

Wolfgang Amadeus Mozart

▲ Ancient Egypt

Ancient Egyptian musicians played harps, rattles and bells while dancers performed in temples and at royal feasts.

Johann Sebastian Bach

►▲ Great composers

In Europe, a great tradition of music developed. Two of the greatest composers were the German Johann Sebastian Bach, who lived from 1685 to 1750, and the Austrian Wolfgang Amadeus Mozart, who lived from 1756 to 1791.

◄ That's jazz!

From the early 1900s, African American bands played a new kind of music called jazz. Players made up some of it as they went along. Louis Armstrong (1901–71) was one of the greatest jazz stars.

Native Americans

Find out more:
Canada ◄ New World ►
United States of America ► Wild West ►

Perhaps as much as 30,000 years ago, hunters from Asia crossed into North America. They were the ancestors (distant relatives) of the Native Americans, the first people to live in what is now the United States. Native American peoples lived by hunting and fishing, and many also became farmers.

birch bark canoe

▲ Travelling light

Around the Great Lakes and rivers of the Midwest, canoes made of birch bark were the best way of travelling.

▼ Plains hunters

Peoples of the Great Plains hunted buffalos which roamed the prairies. Buffalos provided meat and skins for making clothes. People lived in tents called tipis that were also sewn together from buffalo skins.

▲ Troubled times

In the 1800s, more and more settlers of European descent moved into the United States. They called the Native Americans 'Indians'. They stole their land and killed the buffalo. From the 1860s to the 1890s, the Native Americans were defeated in a series of brutal wars.

▲ Ancient ones

A farming people who lived in the canyons of the southwest between about AD500 and 1200 are known as the Anasazi, or 'ancient ones'. By the 1100s, they were living in cliff dwellings, like these ones at Mesa Verde.

New World

Find out more:
African kingdoms ◄ American Revolution ◄ Britain and Ireland ◄
Native Americans ◄ Spain and Portugal ►

In 1492, a European explorer called Christopher Columbus landed in the Americas. He was the first of many. Soon the Spanish and Portuguese were greedily claiming large areas of Central and South America, while the English, Dutch and French were settling in North America. They had discovered a 'New World' of land and natural riches.

▲ Conquistadors

Spanish soldiers called *conquistadors* invaded Mexico in 1519. Their leader was called Hernán Cortés. His forces defeated the Aztec people who lived there.

▲ Pocahontas

Pocahontas lived from 1595 to 1617. She was the daughter of a Native American chief called Powhatan. She tried to make peace between her people and the English, who were settling in Virginia. She married John Rolfe, one of the settlers, but died during a visit to England.

◄ African slaves

In the 1500s, the Europeans started a cruel trade in slaves. People were taken by force from West Africa and shipped to the Americas. There, rich landowners made them work for no money on plantations of sugar or cotton.

Word box

plantation
a piece of land given over to the growing of a particular crop for money

slave
someone whose freedom is taken away and who is forced to work for no money

► The Pilgrims

These English people left Europe because of their strict religious beliefs and so became known as 'pilgrims'. In 1620, they sailed to North America in a ship called *The Mayflower*. They built a new settlement called Plymouth.

New Zealand and the Pacific

Find out more:
Australia ◄
Britain and Ireland ◄

Little islands and coral reefs are scattered over a vast area of the South Pacific Ocean. Over thousands of years they were settled by seafarers. We call these peoples Melanesians, Micronesians and Polynesians. They grew coconuts and sweet potatoes, fished and raised pigs. In the 1800s, many of the islands were settled by Europeans.

▲ The voyagers

The Polynesians originally came from Southeast Asia, sailing in canoes. Between about 1500BC and AD1000 they settled an area of ocean twice the size of the USA.

▲ The Maoris

A Polynesian people called the Maoris reached New Zealand over a thousand years ago. They hunted the big birds that lived there and farmed the land. Maoris continue to live in New Zealand, keeping their traditions and ceremonies alive.

▲ Big heads

In about AD400, the Polynesians sailed from Tahiti to Easter Island. Between 1000 and 1600 they created these huge heads of carved stone on the island.

◄ Wool wagons

In the 1800s, British settlers came to New Zealand for sheep-farming. Here they are using ox-carts to carry bales of wool to market.

Normans

Find out more:
Britain and Ireland ◄ France ◄ Italy ◄ Vikings ►

In the AD900s, the Vikings made many attacks on northern France. The French king decided to buy some peace by giving them land. Their leader, Hrolf, married a French princess called Giselle. This region became known as Normandy ('land of the Northmen') and their descendants were known as Normans.

▼ William the Conqueror

Duke William of Normandy was crowned King of England in London, on Christmas Day 1066. Within two years, most of the country was under Norman rule.

▲ Battle of Hastings

In the summer of 1066, a big Norman fleet arrived on the south coast of England. Their knights attacked the English near Hastings, and killed King Harold II. The Bayeux Tapestry (above) tells the story of the battle.

▲ Domesday Book

The Normans wanted to make the English pay taxes. To do this, they wrote down details of nearly all the land in England. In the 1080s, this information was put together in the Domesday Book.

Wow!

Hrolf, the first Duke of Normandy, was said to be so tall that he could not ride a horse. He was nicknamed 'the ganger', which means 'walker'.

▼ Normans ashore

In 1060, the Normans invaded the island of Sicily, in Italy. They conquered England in 1066, and went on to seize land in Wales and Ireland and to settle in parts of Scotland.

Numbers

Early human beings learned how to count by using their fingers and thumbs. Later, they began to use symbols for different numbers. Mathematics helped ancient peoples count cattle and measure land, work out calendars and plan buildings.

Roman
I II III IV V VI VII VIII IX X

Mayan
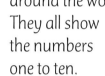

Chinese
一 二 三 四 五 六 七
八 九 十 十五 五十

Indian
१ २ ३ ४ ५ ६ ७ ८ ९ ०

◀ Countdown

Mathematics was studied by the ancient Babylonians, Egyptians, Greeks, Chinese, Arabs and Central Americans. Here are some of the number symbols that developed around the world. They all show the numbers one to ten.

▶ The first calculator

An abacus is a wooden frame with movable beads. These stand for units of tens, hundreds and thousands. The abacus is used for doing sums and was invented in Asia about 5,000 years ago.

▲ Measuring up

The human body was used by the ancient Egyptians to create terms of measurement. A yard was the length of a man's arm. A cubit was the distance between the fingertips and the elbow. A span was the width of an outstretched hand. A foot was the length of a man's foot.

yard

span

cubit

foot

Pirates

The sight every sailor feared was a pirate ship on the horizon.
For thousands of years, pirates robbed ships and attacked or killed their crews. Some pirates were adventurers seeking treasure and thrills. Others were murderers and madmen.

▲ Buccaneers

All sorts of outlaws and criminals settled on the Caribbean islands in the 1600s. These 'buccaneers' lived by hunting wild pigs and by attacking Spanish ships that were laden with treasure from the New World.

▲ Women pirates

Mary Read and Anne Bonny dressed as men and sailed with pirate crews in the Bahamas. The whole crew was captured in 1720 but the women were not executed.

► Blackbeard

Edward Teach, or 'Blackbeard', terrorized the North American coast. He was killed in 1718 and his head was cut off. People believe he buried treasure somewhere before he died. They have been searching for it ever since!

Wow!

When Blackbeard went into battle, he lit the fuses used to fire guns and tied them in his hair. They smoked and fizzled and made him look like the devil!

► Scary flags

Pirate captains flew their own flags, called blackjacks, to strike terror into the enemy.

Religions

As people tried to make sense of the world around them, they came to believe in spirits and gods, in good and in evil. Many of today's world faiths have their origins in Asia. They share some of the same values and ideas.

◀ Jesus

Christians believe that a Jew called Jesus, who lived 2,000 years ago, was the Son of God. They believe he was killed by the Romans, but came back to life and then went to heaven. This picture of Christ was made in Roman Britain, when Christianity was beginning to spread across Europe.

▼ Islam

Muslims believe that there is only one God and that Muhammad is his prophet. Muhammad lived in Arabia between about AD570 and AD632. Ever since, pilgrims have travelled each year to his birthplace, Mecca, shown here.

◀ The Torah

The holy book of the Jews is the Torah, or Law. Jews believe that God gave it to a prophet called Moses over 2,100 years ago.

▲ The Buddha

Siddhartha was a prince who lived from about 563BC to 483BC. He gave up his wealth, declaring that it is worldly desire that makes people unhappy. He became known as the Buddha, which means 'the enlightened one'. Buddhism spread through India, Sri Lanka, China, Japan and Southeast Asia.

Word box

enlightened
seeing the light, or understanding the truth

prophet
someone who speaks the words of God

▶ Hindu beliefs

Hinduism grew up in India over 5,000 years ago. Hindus believe that we are reborn many times. Some believe in many different gods and goddesses, others in one god that appears in various forms.

Religious buildings

Find out more:
African kingdoms ◄ India ◄
Japan and Korea ◄ Religions ◄

Ancient peoples often believed that parts of the landscape, such as mountains or springs, were holy. They soon began to build their own sacred places, too. These included shrines, places of worship such as temples or churches, and monasteries, where monks could live in peace.

▶ Lalibela

This Christian church is in the African country of Ethiopia. It was cut from solid rock nearly 800 years ago. It is in the shape of a Christian cross. In this picture, part of the rock has been cut away, to let you see the whole church.

entrance

▲ Way of the spirits

Traditional Japanese people believe that Mount Fuji is a holy mountain. It rises behind this Shinto shrine. Shinto means the 'way of the spirits' and is based on belief in the powers of nature. It is the most ancient religion in Japan.

▼ All-seeing eyes

Holy mounds called *stupas* have been built by Buddhists in Nepal for over 2,000 years. This one near Kathmandu is decorated with eyes looking north, south, east and west.

Religious symbols

Religions have used special symbols for thousands of years. Can you find out which symbol belongs to which religion?

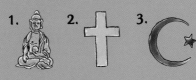

1.   2.   3.

a. Christianity **b.** Islam **c.** Buddhism

answers
1c, 2a, 3b

▼ Golden Temple

This beautiful temple, with its golden roofs and pools of water, is in Amritsar, India. It dates back to the 1500s and is the centre of the Sikh religion.

Renaissance

Between 1350 and 1600 there were many changes in Europe. This period has come to be called the Renaissance, meaning the rebirth. The Renaissance saw a growing interest in science, architecture, poetry, music and art, as well as ancient Greek and Roman culture. Students went to new universities in France, Italy and England.

a model of Leonardo da Vinci's helicopter design

▲ 'Look up!'

Michelangelo, an Italian genius, painted the ceiling of the Sistine Chapel in Rome between 1508 and 1512. Although he had to work on high scaffolding, often lying on his back, everyone agrees that these pictures are some of the best ever painted.

▲ Renaissance man

Leonardo da Vinci lived in Italy from 1452 to 1519. He was a brilliant artist, sculptor, inventor, engineer, architect and musician. This picture is based on a drawing he made of a helicopter. The first modern version, built in 1939, was inspired by his design.

◀ The city of Florence

The Renaissance began in Italy. The wealthy city of Florence became a centre of painting, architecture and sculpture. This is the Duomo, a cathedral that dates from 1296.

▲ New discoveries

The new interest in finding out how things worked led to great scientific discoveries. The Italian scientist Galileo Galilei, who lived from 1564 to 1642, studied the Sun, Moon and planets.

Russia

Find out more:
Byzantine Empire ◄ Kings and queens ◄

Russia is the biggest country in the world. Its western part was settled by a people called the Slavs after about AD400. In the Middle Ages the country was attacked by Mongols, but in the 1500s it united as a single country, with its capital at Moscow.

▼ St Basil's

In the AD800s, monks from the Byzantine Empire brought Christianity to the Slavs. This cathedral, with its colourful onion-shaped domes, is St Basil's, in the centre of Moscow. Building on it began in 1555.

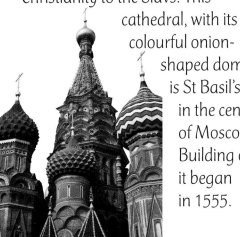

► Catherine the Great

Catherine the Great was empress of Russia from 1762 to 1796. Under her reign, Russia gained many new lands in Europe and Asia.

▲ Revolution, 1917

The tsar (emperor) and nobles in Russia had great power and wealth, while ordinary people had little freedom. Many of them starved. During the 1800s more and more Russians tried to change the way in which their country was ruled. After revolutions in 1917, the communists seized power. They wanted to give power to working people.

► Soviet Union

In 1922, the leader of the Russian Revolution, Lenin (left), founded a new country called the Soviet Union. In 1924, Stalin (right) became leader. Communist rule lasted until 1990, when the Soviet Union started to break up.

Lenin   Stalin

Wow!

When Peter the Great came to the throne in 1682, he hated the long, bushy beards worn by the nobles, so he ordered them all to shave. He even cut some of their beards off himself!

Scandinavia

Find out more:
Holy Roman Empire ◀ Vikings ▶

The far north of Europe is called Scandinavia. It is a snowy land of forests and farmlands, taking in the countries of Norway, Sweden and Denmark. In about AD800, Scandinavia was home to the Vikings. In the later Middle Ages, they set up Christian kingdoms. Sometimes one ruler united the kingdoms, sometimes they were separate countries, as they are today.

▼ Sky watch

This building is an observatory for looking at the stars and planets. It was called *Uraniborg*, meaning 'Castle of the Heavens', and was built in 1576 by a Danish astronomer called Tycho Brahe.

▼ Wooden church

Wooden churches like this one were built in Norway during the Middle Ages. The Christian faith first reached Norway during the reign of King Olaf I, between AD995 and 1000.

Word scramble

Can you unscramble these children's stories? They were all written by Hans Christian Andersen in the 1800s:

a. **EHT YGLU GLINKCUD**
b. **HET WONS NEQUE**
c. **TEH NIT RODLIES**
d. **HET SROMPREE WEN SETHCOL**

answers
a. *The Ugly Duckling*
b. *The Snow Queen*
c. *The Tin Soldier*
d. *The Emperor's New Clothes*

▲ A battling king

In the 1600s, Sweden was one of the most powerful countries in Europe. It fought against the Holy Roman Empire during the Thirty Years War. The Swedes won the Battle of Lützen in 1632, but their king, Gustavus Adolphus, was killed in the fighting.

▼ The Little Mermaid

This statue in Copenhagen, Denmark, shows the Little Mermaid, from the famous story by Hans Christian Andersen. This author, who lived from 1805 to 1875, wrote many famous children's tales.

Schools

Find out more:
Ancient Egyptian life ◄ Ancient Roman life ◄ Canada ◄
Numbers ◄ Writing and printing ►

In the Stone Age, children were taught how to hunt or gather food by their parents. As people learned to write and do sums, children needed all sorts of new lessons, with teachers and proper schools. Often it was only the boys from rich families who were sent to school. Girls stayed at home and learned how to cook or sew.

▲ Class of 1898

This class was photographed in Canada in 1898. By then, education was beginning to spread and poor children, including girls, started going to school.

► Learning to read

In the 1500s, English school children learned to read letters and standard sentences on this hand-held panel, called a 'hornbook'.

▲ In ancient Egypt

Egyptian boys went to school each morning. They learned to do sums and practised their writing on broken bits of pottery. They were expected to behave well and were beaten if they misbehaved.

► Roman lessons

Roman children learned arithmetic. They learned to read and write in Greek, as well as in their own language, Latin. Older pupils were taught history, poetry and how to speak well in public.

Word box

arithmetic
a kind of mathematics that involves doing sums

education
teaching and learning

How does the world work? What is it made of? What are living things and how do they behave? Questions like these have interested human beings for thousands of years. At first they looked to magic or to their gods for explanations. From the 1600s onwards, scientists began to work out many of the true answers.

► Marie Curie

Marie Curie was a brilliant Polish woman who lived from 1867 to 1934. She lived in France, where she studied magnetism and the useful, but dangerous, rays given out by some metals.

◄ Why do things fall?

Around 1665, an English scientist called Isaac Newton watched an apple drop from a tree in his garden. He began to study gravity, the invisible force that tugs everything on Earth downwards. He also studied light and made new kinds of telescope.

Word box

magnetism
the force that pulls two objects together, such as a magnet and a piece of iron

Universe
the stars, planets, space and everything that exists

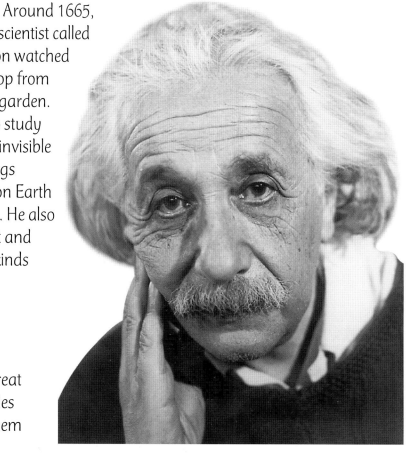

► Brain power

Albert Einstein was born in Germany in 1867. He later lived in Switzerland and the USA. He was a great mathematician and worked out astonishing theories about the Universe and how it worked. Many of them have since been proved to be true.

Space and air travel

Find out more:
Transport on land ▶   Transport on water ▶

In ancient times, people longed to fly like a bird across the sky, or even travel to the Moon. Few believed that these things would ever happen. Today, our planes can fly vast distances in just a few hours and we can send spacecraft far beyond our Solar System.

▲ Above the waves

Planes like this one were made in the 1930s and 1940s. They could land and take off on water and so were called flying boats.

▲ Hot air balloon

If you heat air, it rises up. Two French brothers called Joseph and Jacques Montgolfier designed large balloons filled with hot air. The first balloon flight with passengers took place in 1783.

▲ Atlantic flight

The first plane to cross the Atlantic Ocean was a Vickers-Vimy, flown by John William Alcock and Arthur Whitten Brown. It flew from Newfoundland to Ireland in 1919, taking 16 hours and 27 minutes.

Word box

astronaut
a man or woman who is trained to travel in space

Solar System
our Sun and all the planets and moons that travel around it

▲ Moon mission

The *Saturn V* rocket was designed in the USA to launch the *Apollo* missions to the Moon in the 1960s and 1970s.

Wow!

A Russian astronaut called Yuri Gagarin was the first man to travel in space, in 1961. He circled the Earth at speeds of 28,260 kilometres an hour!

Spain and Portugal

Find out more:
Explorers at sea ◀ New World ◀

Spain and Portugal were invaded and settled by all sorts of peoples, including Basques, Iberians, Celts, Greeks, Romans, Germans, Moors, Jews and Roma (gypsies). In the 1500s, the kingdoms of Spain and Portugal conquered lands in the New World, making both countries rich and powerful. Spain ruled Portugal from 1586 to 1646.

▲ The navigators

This statue in Lisbon, Portugal, recalls the Portuguese explorers of the 1400s, such as Bartolomeu Díaz and Vasco da Gama. They were some of the first Europeans to carry out long sea voyages, sailing around the coast of Africa and crossing the Indian Ocean.

▶ El Cid

The Spanish knight Ruy Díaz de Vivar was a hero of the Middle Ages. He fought against, and sometimes with, the Moors who lived in southern Spain. They called him *El Cid*, which means 'the lord'. In 1094, he captured Valencia and became its ruler.

Ferdinand of Aragon

Isabella of Castile

◀ Ferdinand and Isabella

Christian knights defeated the Muslim Moors and in 1479 Spain became one country under the rule of Isabella of Castile and Ferdinand of Aragon.

◀ Spanish rebels

Between 1936 and 1939, Spain was shattered by a bloody civil war. General Franco then ruled as a dictator until 1975, when Juan Carlos I became king and a fair government was established.

Word box

Moor
a Muslim of Berber or Arab descent, who lived in Morocco or Spain in the Middle Ages

Sport

People have always enjoyed playing and watching sports. In the ancient world, games were sometimes part of important religious festivals. Athletics helped to train warriors for war, too, and to keep them fit. Ancient Greek weapons, such as the javelin, are still thrown by athletes today.

▼ The Olympic Games

In 1906, the first of the modern series of the Olympic Games was held in Athens, Greece. The original games had been held between 771 BC and AD 393. Ancient events included discus-throwing, running, jumping and wrestling.

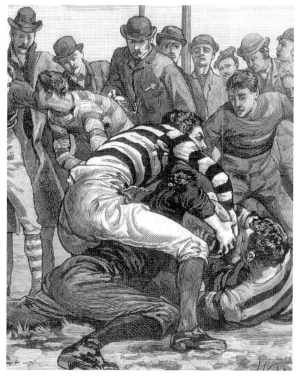

1906   771 BC

▲ Making up the rules

Rugby football was invented in 1823 by a schoolboy who picked up a football and ran with it. Many other sports became popular in the 1800s and were given proper rules. These included lawn tennis, netball, badminton and baseball.

Support your team!

What is your favourite team sport and which team do you follow?

See if you can find out the facts below. Then make a chart that you can stick up on the wall, and decorate it with club colours and badges.

1. When was your favourite sport first played?
2. Where was the sport first played?
3. When was your team founded?
4. Which year was the most successful in its history?
5. Who was its best player ever?

▼ Speed sports

New machines meant new and ever faster sports were taken up in the 1900s. Racing cycles, motorcycles, cars and aeroplanes now pulled in big crowds of spectators. These racing cars date from 1953.

Stone Age

Find out more:
Farming ◄ Housing and shelter ◄
Ice ages ◄

Before people learned how to make things from metal, they made tools and weapons from stone, shell, wood, horn or bone. This period is called the Stone Age. Copper was being worked in some parts of Asia and Europe by 6000BC, but it took thousands of years for these metal-working skills to spread.

► Survival

The Stone Age lasted tens of thousands of years. Although people knew less than we do today, they could be just as clever. They worked out ever better ways of hunting, fishing and gathering food. In the end, they learned how to farm.

▲ Ring of stone

Towards the end of the Stone Age in Britain, some people created a ring of massive stones at Stonehenge. The stones were lined up to follow the path of the Sun across the sky. Historians think that important religious ceremonies were held here between about 3200BC and 1100BC.

▼ Homes for the dead

Between about 5,700 and 4,000 years ago, important people in northwestern Europe were buried in stone tombs, covered with mounds of earth. Some of these tombs, called barrows, can still be visited today.

▲ Cutting edge

Stone Age tools included scrapers, knives, axe-heads, spear-heads, arrows and fish-hooks. Many were made from a hard stone called flint, which could be chipped into the right shape.

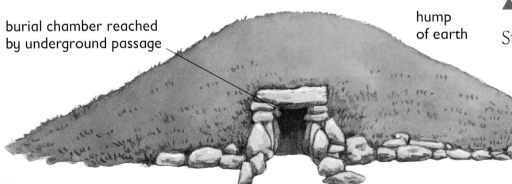

burial chamber reached by underground passage

hump of earth

Theatre and cinema

Find out more:
Art in history ◀   Music and dance ◀

The sound of clapping and laughter or gasps of fear are all part of watching a play. Drama dates back thousands of years. It often had its beginnings in religious ceremonies and was linked with the arts, such as dance, music or story-telling.

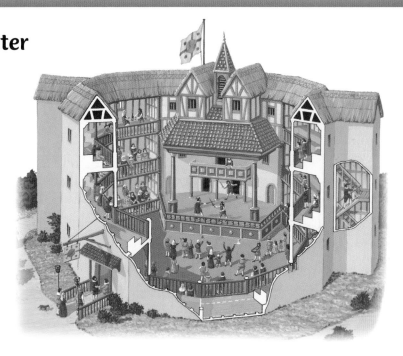

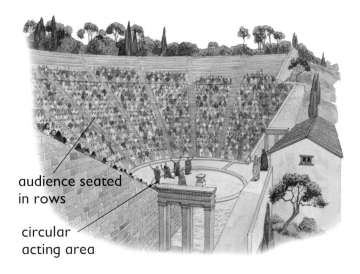

audience seated in rows

circular acting area

▲ Greek theatre

The ancient Greeks built open-air theatres so that people could watch plays together. Many plays were written in Greek between 400BC and 500BC – some were comedies and some tragedies. Many are still performed today.

Word box

comedy
a funny play

drama
performing a story or play in a theatre

tragedy
a sad play

▲ Shakespeare's age

This is what an English theatre looked like 400 years ago. Some of the audience sat on balconies, while others stood in the yard. They shouted and ate during the performance. Some of the most popular plays were by William Shakespeare, who lived from 1564 to 1616, and was one of the world's greatest writers of plays.

▶ Demons and gods

An ancient kind of theatre can be seen outside Hindu temples in Kerala, India. The performers, all male, play demons and gods. They wear colourful costumes and make-up that looks like a mask.

◀ What a Charlie!

Cinema became popular in the 1900s. The first films were silent. Charlie Chaplin, who began making films in 1914, was much loved all over the world. He played the part of a tramp who was always getting into trouble.

Time

People have always needed to record the passing of time. Calendars of the seasons were made in ancient times in Asia and the Americas. These helped people know when to sow or plant crops. People also worked out ways to count off the hours during the day.

▶ Clockwork

Clocks were invented in China in the AD700s. By 1310, clocks were also being made in Europe. This fancy clock dates from around 1400 and stands in Prague, in the Czech Republic.

▼ Sundial

The sundial is believed to have been used in Babylon at least as early as 2000BC. As the Sun moved across the sky during the day, it cast a shadow on the flat dial, which was marked to show the time. The trouble was, it could only show the time on a sunny day.

▲ The hour glass

As a measured amount of time passes, sand pours from the top glass into the bottom one. The same design is used for egg-timers.

Wow!

In the days before radio and trains, each town told its time from the local clock. There might be ten minutes difference between the time in one city and another.

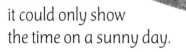

◄ 'Do you have the time?'

Beautiful pocket watches were being produced in Germany after about 1500. However, the very first wristwatch was Swiss and dates from 1790. This shows a typical pocket watch, based on the original Swiss design.
▼

Toys

Find out more:
Ancient Egyptian life ◄ Ancient Greek cities ◄
Ancient Roman life ◄ Victorian Britain ►

Children in the Stone Age probably played with pebbles, seeds, shells, feathers, toy spears and clay figures. Dolls, toys and other games have survived from ancient Egypt and we know that toys were sold at fairs in the Middle Ages. In the 1800s, cheap toys made of tin or wood were made in factories.

◄ Egyptian toys

Children in ancient Egypt played with colourful balls made from linen and rags, spinning tops, dolls and toy lions whose jaws snapped when they pulled a string.

▼ Dice and marbles

The ancient Romans loved playing dice and had many board games with their own pieces or counters.

▼ Rocking horses

In the days when everyone rode about on horseback, little children played with hobbyhorses and wheeled wooden horses. Rocking horses were first made in the 1600s. This one dates from the 1800s.

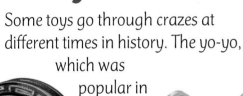

▼ Yo-yo!

Some toys go through crazes at different times in history. The yo-yo, which was popular in the 1930s, 1950s and 1990s, was also a toy in ancient Greece.

► Teddy

Teddy bears were first made 100 years ago. They probably take their name from an American president called 'Teddy' Roosevelt, who is said to have spared the life of a little bear when he was out hunting.

Wow!

The oldest board game surviving today was played by Sumerians at the royal court of Ur, over 4,500 years ago.

Transport on land

For thousands of years people travelled on horseback or in slow carts pulled by oxen or horses. In the frozen north, sleds and sleighs were used to cross snow. In the 1800s, new kinds of transport were invented, powered by steam, petrol and electricity. They changed the world.

▼ Coach travel

Horse-drawn coaches began to be widely used in Europe in the 1500s and 1600s. The roads were muddy and full of holes, so the passengers had a bumpy and uncomfortable journey.

▲ On your bike!

This was the first proper bicycle. It had pedals that pushed rods. These drove the back wheel round and round. Kirkpatrick Macmillan, a Scot, invented the bicycle in 1839.

Trevithick's steam engine

◄ Pulling power

In 1803, the very first steam locomotive pulled wagons along a railway track in Wales. It was built by an engineer called Richard Trevithick.

▼ Motor cars

The first car with a petrol engine was built in 1885 by Karl Benz. It had three wheels. The design of cars improved rapidly, so that, by the 1900s, motor cars were popular, if expensive.

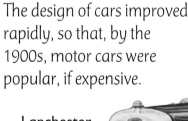

Lanchester

Wow!

Before 1896, the speed limit on British roads was 6 kilometres an hour. Even so, this was thought to be so dangerous that a man with a red warning flag had to walk in front of each car!

Transport on water

Find out more:
Explorers at sea ◄ Space and air travel ◄
Transport on land ◄

The remains of a wooden canoe found in the Netherlands are over 9,000 years old. The Egyptians were building ships with sails by 5,000 years ago. Steam power began to replace sail power in the 1800s, and ships were now made of iron instead of wood.

► The big liners

Luxurious steam-powered passenger ships were built during the 1900s. They were called 'liners' after the shipping lines that owned them. This is the *Queen Mary*, one of the great liners of the 1930s.

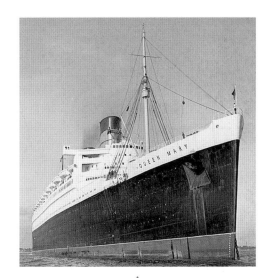

▲ Wind power

This ship has been built in the style of the late 1800s, when sail power was at its height. Merchant ships were very fast, covering vast distances in a matter of days.

► Paddling along

Big paddle wheels at the back or sides drove the first steamboats along. In the 1800s, riverboats like these were seen on rivers in the USA.

▲ Trading ship

Ships such as these could use oars as well as sails. The Romans used them to transport people and cargo across the sea and along rivers.

Tudors and Stuarts

In the 1500s and 1600s, Britain was ruled by two powerful families, the Tudors and the Stuarts (or Stewarts). This was a time of bitter quarrels between Christians. The Roman Catholics supported the Pope in Rome, but the Protestants wanted to break away from the Roman Church.

▲ Henry VIII (Henry the Eighth)

The Tudors reigned over England and Wales from 1485 to 1603. Henry VIII was desperate for a son to succeed him. When the Pope refused to give him a divorce from his first wife, Henry made himself head of a new Church of England.

▼ Two queens

During troubled times in Scotland, Mary Stuart, Queen of Scots, fled to England. After being tried for plotting against Elizabeth I (below), Mary had her head chopped off.

◄ A Tudor town house

This fine house was built by a wealthy businessman in the town of Conwy, Wales, in 1577. It was built in the shape of an 'E', after Elizabeth I.

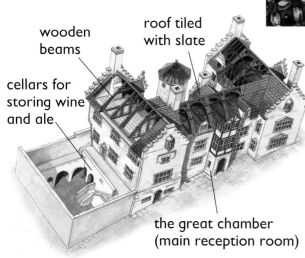

wooden beams

roof tiled with slate

cellars for storing wine and ale

the great chamber (main reception room)

▲ Country at war

King Charles I was unpopular. A war broke out between his supporters and the English Parliament. They cut his head off in 1649 and in 1653 handed over power to a soldier called Oliver Cromwell, who ruled the country for the next five years.

▼ King of Scotland

The Stuarts (or Stewarts) ruled Scotland for most of the time between 1371 and 1714. This is James IV (James the Fourth), one of the greatest Scottish kings. He was killed fighting the English in 1513. In 1603, the Stuarts came to rule England too.

Turkey

A Turkish people called the Ottomans captured Constantinople in 1453. They founded a new empire which soon spread across Turkey, Greece and southeastern Europe, Arabia, Egypt and North Africa. The Ottoman Empire finally came to an end in 1922 and Turkey became a republic. It still has more people living there than any other country in western Asia.

▲► New Turkey

The Turks were defeated in 1918, at the close of World War One. The country was built up again by a man called Mustapha Kemal Atatürk, who was president from 1923 to 1938.

► Topkapi

During the 1460s and 1470s, the grand new palace of Topkapi Sarayi was built in Istanbul, looking out over the sea. At times, as many as 5,000 people lived in the palace buildings.

◄ Istanbul

The Turks turned Constantinople into the Muslim city of Istanbul. The graceful Blue Mosque was built for Sultan Ahmet I. It was finally finished in 1619.

Word box

republic
a country that is not ruled by a king or queen

sultan
the king of a Muslim country

► Magnificent!

The Ottoman Empire reached the height of its power under a ruler or 'sultan' called Süleyman I, the Magnificent, who died in 1566. His armies marched westwards as far as Austria.

United States of America

Find out more:
American Revolution ◄
Native Americans ◄ Wild West ►

In the 1800s, the new country of the USA grew very quickly. It gained lands in the South, the Southwest, California and Alaska. New settlers arrived from Ireland, Italy, Germany, Poland and Russia. Despite a civil war and battles with the Native Americans, farming and factories flourished. By the 1950s, the USA had become the richest and most powerful nation in the world.

▲ North v. South

In 1861, 11 southern states withdrew from the Union that made up the USA. They disagreed about the way in which the country was to be governed and they wanted to keep slavery. Many people died in this bitter civil war, which lasted until 1865, when the Union won.

Martin Luther King Junior

► Statue of Liberty

Many Europeans came to America between 1850 and 1910 in search of a better, fairer life. The Statue of Liberty was a gift from the French people to the United States in 1884. It was a symbol of this fairness and freedom.

◄ 'I have a dream...'

One hundred years after the end of slavery, African Americans were still being treated as second-class citizens in the USA. Martin Luther King Junior led a campaign for justice. In a famous speech, he told people that he had a dream of a land in which all people were free and equal. He was killed in 1968.

▼ Abraham Lincoln

Abraham Lincoln was president of the USA from 1861 to 1865, when he was murdered. He was a great leader who helped to bring slavery to an end.

Victorian Britain

Find out more:
Britain and Ireland ◄ Empires and colonies ◄
Industrial Revolution ◄

From 1837 to 1901, Britain was ruled by Queen Victoria. Her reign is called the Victorian Age. She ruled over large areas of the world, which made up the biggest empire in history. At this time Britain led the world in trade and in building new factories.

▶ Crystal Palace

In 1851, a huge glass building called the Crystal Palace was put up in Hyde Park, London. Inside it was the Great Exhibition, organized by Prince Albert. It showed off produce, crafts and new machines from all over the world.

▼ A long reign

Queen Victoria was only 18 when she came to the throne, and she ruled for 63 years. She married a German prince called Albert. His death, in 1861, made her very sad.

◄ Ladies of fashion

Victorian ladies wore full dresses that were stretched over a hooped petticoat called a crinoline. These 1870s models are showing off the bustle, a pad which pushed out the back of the skirt.

▼ The poor

Many people in Victorian Britain were extremely poor. Their lives were described in stories by the great writer Charles Dickens, who lived from 1812 to 1870.

Be a Victorian fashion designer

1. Draw a Victorian lady in a dress and bonnet, like the ones shown in the picture above.
2. Colour in her costume and add patterns, lace and bows.

Vikings

Find out more:
Normans ◄ Scandinavia ◄

The word 'Viking' means sea raider. About 1,200 years ago, Vikings caused terror along the coasts of northern Europe. They sailed from Norway, Sweden and Denmark to attack, plunder and settle new lands. They traded as far away as Russia and the Middle East. They even sailed to Iceland, Greenland and North America.

▲ Meeting up

All free Viking men gathered regularly at a special meeting called the Thing. There they passed new laws and settled any arguments between them.

▶ Life at home

The Vikings built farming settlements, ports and towns. They were great craft workers, traders and storytellers. Family life took place around the fire.

▲ Northern fury

Viking chiefs lead a band of raiders ashore from their longboat, armed with spears, swords and axes. Viking warriors attacked towns and Christian monasteries, seizing gold, silver, cattle and weapons. Sometimes they captured people to sell as slaves.

▶ Thor's hammer

The Vikings believed in different gods and goddesses. Thor, god of thunder, had a magic hammer that he used to fight giants. His chariot was pulled by goats.

Make a Viking treasure hoard

1. Make some coins by cutting out circles of card. Viking coins might be stamped with designs of ships or swords. Cover your coins with silver foil then use a blunt pencil to make a design on them.
2. Cut out a cross and a brooch from card. Again, cover with foil and press a design on them.

Wild West

In the 1840s, the Europeans who had settled in the eastern United States began to move westwards. They settled on the prairies (grasslands) and seized land from the Native Americans. They planted crops and kept cattle, working as cowboys. Some went all the way across to the Pacific coast, in search of land or the glint of gold.

Word scramble

Can you unscramble these names? They all belong to famous people from the Wild West:

a. MALACITY ENJA
b. TAWTY PERA
c. ENNIA KEOLAY

answers
a. Calamity Jane b. Wyatt Earp c. Annie Oakley

▲ The Oregon Trail

Covered wagons took whole families westwards from Missouri, often as far as Oregon. It was a rough ride and many travellers died from accidents or lack of water.

▲ Buffalo Bill

William Cody was an army scout and buffalo hunter. In 1883, he set up a spectacular 'Wild West Show', which went on tour. In the 1900s, film-makers took up the same story of outlaws, cowboys and 'Indians' (as Native Americans were known).

◀ Lawless times

Gunfights and robbery were all too common. William Bonney was a cattle thief who killed 21 men before he was shot, in 1881. He was better known as 'Billy the Kid'.

◀ The 'Forty-Niners'

In 1849, gold was discovered in California. Prospectors (gold hunters) rushed to 'stake a claim', marking out their own area. They then set up camp and started searching for traces of gold in the rivers.

Women's rights

Find out more:
World War One ▶ World War Two ▶

In the late 1800s, many women in Europe and North America were angry. They did not have the same rights as men and could not vote in elections. They were badly paid in factories and mills. Often they were not allowed to go to university or to be doctors or judges. They demanded better lives.

Nancy Astor

◀ Into parliament

The first nation to allow women to vote was New Zealand, in 1893. Nancy Astor became Britain's first female Member of Parliament, in 1919. Times were changing.

▼ 'Votes for women!'

Women who campaigned for the vote in the 1900s were called suffragists or suffragettes. They protested by breaking windows and chaining themselves to railings. Many were sent to prison.

▲ Wars and work

Many men had to go away to fight in wars from 1914 to 1918 and 1939 to 1945. Women were taken on to do work that only men had done before. They worked on farms or in factories. They proved that they were just as good as men, but they were still not paid as much.

◀ Bloomers

Amelia Bloomer was an American who campaigned for a better deal for women in the 1850s. She wanted them to wear more practical clothes, so she invented a new kind of trousers. These became known as 'bloomers'.

World War One

Find out more:
World War Two ▶

A terrible war broke out in 1914. It was fought in many different parts of the world, so it later became known as a World War. The Central Powers, which included Germany, Austria and Turkey, fought against the Allies, which in the end included the British Empire, France, Russia, Italy, Japan and the USA. Peace did not come until 1918.

▲ New weapons

Terrible new weapons were invented during World War One. The Allies used armoured tanks, like these. The Central Powers attacked their enemies with poisonous gas.

▼ War in the air

Planes were now used to fly over the enemy, spying out the land, or dropping bombs. This German plane had three wings.

▲ In the trenches

The opposing armies faced each other along a line which stretched from Belgium to Switzerland. Soldiers sheltered in long trenches dug into the ground, defended by barbed wire.

◄ So many dead

Ambulances such as this one carried wounded soldiers from the scene of battle. By 1918, ten million soldiers had been killed and many more injured.

Word box

barbed wire
tangled wire fitted with sharp spikes

poisonous gas
gas that poisoned anyone who breathed it in

tanks
armoured vehicles with moving tracks instead of wheels

trench
a deep ditch, dug to shelter soldiers from gunfire

a b c d e f g h i j k l m n o p q r s t u v **w** x y z   **91**

A second World War broke out in 1939 and lasted until 1945. In the end, armies from the British Empire, the Soviet Union (Russia) and the USA defeated those of Germany, Italy and Japan. This was the worst war in human history, leaving 55 million soldiers and civilians dead around the world.

▼ The Nazis

During World War Two, Germany was ruled by the Nazi Party. Their leader was Adolf Hitler. Anyone who disagreed with the Nazis was put in prison or killed. The Nazis hated Jewish people and set up death camps, where six million people were murdered.

◄ Pearl Harbor

In 1941, Japanese planes attacked an American naval base at Pearl Harbor, in Hawaii. The USA now entered the war, fighting in the Pacific islands and across Europe.

Word box

civilian
someone who is not serving as a soldier, sailor or airman

▲ Fast warfare

Germany invaded most of Europe, while Japanese troops advanced quickly through East and Southeast Asia. World War Two weapons included high-speed tanks, dive-bombers and deadly submarines.

► Cities bombed

Many cities all over Britain and Germany were devastated by bombs. Here, thick smoke hangs over the city of London in 1940. St Paul's Cathedral is surrounded by blazing buildings.

Writing and printing

Writing began about 5,500 years ago, in the Middle East. It allowed people to keep records and to write down their stories for the people who came after them. All sorts of scripts came into use around the world, from China to Central America. They included patterns, pictures, symbols and alphabets. These signs stood for objects, ideas or sounds.

▶ A B C D...

Alphabets are made up of letters that stand for different sounds. The alphabet used in this book grew from those used in southwest Asia and southern Europe. Here are the first six letters of nine different alphabets and scripts.

Phoenician

Classical Greek

Roman
A B C D E F

Cyrillic
А Б В Г Д Е

Hebrew

Arabic

Ancient Egyptian

Chinese
人 月 子 水 雨 木

Japanese
星 面 海 水 下

▼ Picture writing

Between about 3200BC and AD400, Egyptian priests used a kind of writing made up of picture symbols called hieroglyphs. These can still be seen on the walls of old tombs or written out on papyrus.

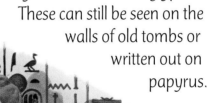

▲ Printed books

This Buddhist holy book was printed by hand in AD868, using carved wooden blocks to make the words and pictures.

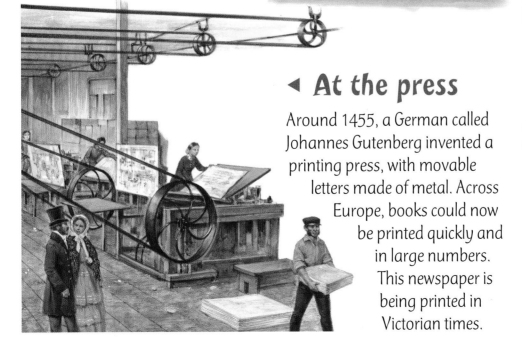

◀ At the press

Around 1455, a German called Johannes Gutenberg invented a printing press, with movable letters made of metal. Across Europe, books could now be printed quickly and in large numbers. This newspaper is being printed in Victorian times.

Word box

papyrus
a kind of paper made from reeds

printing press
a machine in which metal shapes covered in ink are pressed against a page to print words or pictures

script
signs that are used in writing

Index

The numbers in **bold** type refer to main entries in your book

**The publishers would like to thank
the following artists who have contributed
to this book:**
Richard Berridge, Steve Caldwell, Vanessa Card,
Mark Davis, Peter Dennis, Nicholas Forder,
Terry Gabbey, Luigi Galante, Peter Gregory,
Alan Hancocks, Sally Holmes, Richard Hook,
John James, Aziz Khan, Andy Lloyd Jones,
Kevin Maddison, Maltings Partnership,
Janos Marffy, Angus McBride, Roger Payne,
Terry Riley, Pete Roberts, Eric Rowe, Martin Sanders,
Peter Sarson, Mike Saunders, Rob Sheffield,
Guy Smith, Nik Spender, Roger Stewart,
Mark Taylor, Rudi Vizi, Mike White, John Woodcock

**The publishers would like to thank the
following for supplying photographs for
this book:**
AFP: 68 (c); Roger_Viollet/AFP 18 (c/l);
British Library/The Art Archive: 93 (c/l);
Corbis: Bettmann 72 (t/r); Historical Picture
Archive 87 (t/r); Hulton-Deutsch Collection 23 (c/b),
64 (c/b), 85 (c); Earl Kowall 17 (b/r);
Bob Krist 72 (b/l)